Crowdfunding and Independence in Film and Music

This book explores how independent film and music artists and labels use crowdfunding and where this use places crowdfunding in the contemporary system of cultural production. It complements an analysis of independence in film and music with the topic of crowdfunding as a firmly established form of financing cultural activity.

In the second half of the 20th century, the concept of artistic independence was vital to classifying and distinguishing artists, their works, and labels or publishers who released them. However, during the last three decades, this term has become increasingly blurred, and some commentators argue that independence is in crisis. Can crowdfunding be the answer to this crisis? Some believe that it is, whereas others argue otherwise, seeing crowdfunding instead as just the next manifestation of this crisis. This dilemma is a starting point for the analyses of the relationships between crowdfunding and artistic independence conducted in this book, and will be of great interest to people looking for a deeper understanding of crowdfunding, how it can influence artistic independence, and what it means for artists and audiences.

It will be a stimulating read for scholars and students with an interest in media and cultural studies, digital humanities, fandom, sociology, economics, business studies, and law, while also offering insights to artists and practitioners in the creative industries.

Blanka Brzozowska is Associate Professor at the Institute of Contemporary Culture at the University of Lodz, Poland.

Patryk Galuszka is Associate Professor in the Faculty of Economics and Sociology at the University of Lodz, Poland.

Routledge Focus on Media and Cultural Studies

Community Media and Identity in Ireland
Jack Rosenberry

Cultural Chauvinism
Intercultural Communication and the Politics of Superiority
Minabere Ibelema

Crowdfunding and Independence in Film and Music
Blanka Brzozowska and Patryk Galuszka

Crowdfunding and Independence in Film and Music

Blanka Brzozowska
and Patryk Galuszka

LONDON AND NEW YORK

First published 2021
by Routledge
2 Park Square, Milton Park, Abingdon, Oxon OX14 4RN

and by Routledge
605 Third Avenue, New York, NY 10158

Routledge is an imprint of the Taylor & Francis Group, an informa business

© 2021 Blanka Brzozowska and Patryk Galuszka

The right of Blanka Brzozowska and Patryk Galuszka to be identified as authors of this work has been asserted by them in accordance with sections 77 and 78 of the Copyright, Designs, and Patents Act 1988.

All rights reserved. No part of this book may be reprinted or reproduced or utilized in any form or by any electronic, mechanical, or other means, now known or hereafter invented, including photocopying and recording, or in any information storage or retrieval system, without permission in writing from the publishers.

Trademark notice: Product or corporate names may be trademarks or registered trademarks, and are used only for identification and explanation without intent to infringe.

British Library Cataloguing-in-Publication Data
A catalogue record for this book is available from the British Library

Library of Congress Cataloging-in-Publication Data
A catalog record has been requested for this book

ISBN: 978-0-367-71406-2 (hbk)
ISBN: 978-0-367-71414-7 (pbk)
ISBN: 978-1-003-15078-7 (ebk)

Typeset in Times New Roman
by MPS Limited, Dehradun

Contents

Note on Authors		vi
Acknowledgments		vii
1	Introduction	1
2	Crowdfunding as a new form of financing creative activity	5
3	Crowdfunding independent cinema	18
4	Crowdfunding and independence in music	62
5	Conclusions	96
	References	103
	Index	114

Note on Authors

Blanka Brzozowska is Associate Professor at the Institute of Contemporary Culture at the University of Lodz. Her research interests include digital media and cultural studies. Her current research projects concentrate on crowdfunding, embodied and play design, and urban cultures in the context of social media development. She has published in such journals as *Creativity Studies, Media, Culture & Society, International Journal of Communication, International Journal of Cultural Studies*, and *Continuum: Journal of Media & Cultural Studies*.

Patryk Galuszka is Associate Professor in the Faculty of Economics and Sociology at the University of Lodz. He conducts research on music industries and the influence of new communication technologies on artists' careers. His recent work concentrates on crowdfunding, music streaming, and internationalization of the Polish recording industry. He has published in such journals as *Media, Culture & Society, International Journal of Communication, International Journal of Cultural Studies, Popular Music & Society, Popular Music,* and *Continuum: Journal of Media & Cultural Studie*s. His most recent works are edited volumes: *Made in Poland: Studies in Popular Music* (Routledge, 2020) and *Eastern European Music Industries and Policies after the Fall of Communism: From State Control to Free Market* (Routledge, 2021).

Acknowledgments

The research for this book was supported by the National Science Center, Poland (grant number 2015/17/B/HS6/04150).

We would like to thank our colleague Kamila Zyto who supported us with critical reading and interesting discussions about independent cinema.

1 Introduction

In 2012, Amanda Palmer raised $1.2 million on the Kickstarter crowdfunding platform, 12 times more than the campaign's target. Her campaign was hailed as a breakthrough (to this day, no musician has raised as much on this platform), and it attracted substantial media attention, drawn both to the artist herself and to the idea of musicians using crowdfunding. Palmer repeatedly emphasized that she considered crowdfunding a great tool, one that enabled an artist to function independently of the (traditional) recording industry. However, after the success of the campaign, and partly as a result of it, Palmer faced a series of public relations failures. One of the largest of these resulted from an invitation via social media to musicians in cities that she visited during the promotional tour for her new album to perform on stage. The proposal was worded as follows: "We will feed you beer, hug/high-five you up and down (pick your poison), give you merch, and thank you mightily for adding to the big noise we are planning to make" (Ronson 2013, n.p.). It did not include remuneration, which, given the awareness that the initiator had just beaten the Kickstarter collection record, caused considerable controversy. Palmer's explanation that she "immediately spent all that money on the packaging and the mailing, and it was all gone six weeks later" (Ronson 2013, n.p.) was not accepted with understanding.

The case of Amanda Palmer is a spectacular example of the use of crowdfunding and highlights concerns associated with this form of financing for creative activity. How should Amanda Palmer's Kickstarter campaign be understood? As a fulfillment of dreams of artistic independence after a two-year battle with a record label to terminate her contract? Or perhaps as an attempt to capitalize on a fan base built earlier, while working with the label? Were the controversies that arose after the success of the campaign merely public relations errors, or were they a manifestation of a disagreement as to how creativity should be financed in the increasingly dominant social media?

Finding answers to these questions requires looking at the space crowdfunding occupies in the current ecosystem of creative industries and considering how it can be used. However, we should emphasize here that the use of crowdfunding by Amanda Palmer, although fascinating, should not be considered an illustration of every aspect of the use of crowdfunding by artists, as there is no single type of crowdfunding, and not every artist using it is in the same situation as Amanda Palmer was. Crowdfunding is an umbrella term that includes different approaches to raising capital on platforms that are often governed by different rules. There are also significant differences among the cultural products financed by crowdfunding. For example, crowdfunding of a music project differs from that of a film project – in most cases, differences lie in the amount of money sought and the ways in which campaigns are run by their initiators. It is impossible to draw far-reaching conclusions from a single case for such a diverse and rapidly changing phenomenon as crowdfunding. Therefore, though we will return to the case of Amanda Palmer, we will focus on a broader context, illustrated by lesser known but analytically significant examples of the use of crowdfunding.

The objective of this book is to analyze how crowdfunding is used by independent artists, with particular focus on two areas of activity, film and music, and to reflect on the place of crowdfunding in the contemporary system of cultural production. Two issues should be clarified here. First, why focus on independent artists, given the ambiguity the term "independence" has acquired over the last two decades? Abandoning the term "independent" would allow us to take more cases into account and to avoid the need to discuss the ambiguous and difficult-to-define concept of artistic independence. The answer to this question can be divided into two parts. On the one hand, crowdfunding is superb at financing projects that most experts would agree are independent. Crowdfunding gives artists, or those who want to keep as much control over their work as possible, possibilities that their predecessors in the 1960s and 1970s could only dream of. On the other hand, the independence of crowdfunding is often idealized. Crowdfunding imposes significant restrictions on artists who want to maintain their independence, sometimes in ways that are different from those used in the traditional corporate-financing model. What is more, this form of financing is not the exclusive domain of independent artists; it is also used by mainstream artists and corporations. Although crowdfunding is a vital tool for many independent artists, its relationship with artistic independence is complicated.

The second issue to be clarified is the selection of film and music as the areas of activity for analysis. Why not other creative activities often financed by crowdfunding, such as art or design? The fact that we study these two areas of creative activity in our daily academic work has of course influenced our choice. More importantly, in music and film, independence has for decades been a key criterion in the perception and interpretation of creativity. What is more, in the last dozen or so years the notion of independence has become somewhat blurred, especially in music. If we are to look for a place where independence can be manifested today and thanks to which it can be realized, it is crowdfunding. While independent music and film are not the only activities that are developing as a result of crowdfunding (video games are another example), this form of financing has given them a new impulse that has the potential to partially overcome the dilemmas faced by independent artists.

We have taken these dilemmas into account in the structure of this book. Our task is, on the one hand, to explain what crowdfunding culture is and how it works, using the examples of film and music. At the same time, we address a number of doubts related to perceptions of crowdfunding as a tool enabling artists to maintain or regain their independence. Moreover, our analysis is carried out in a situation where the concept of independence is perceptibly abused. Both Jonathan Coulton, who does not cooperate with any music label and the majority of whose works are released under Creative Commons licenses, and Trent Reznor (of Nine Inch Nails), who built his position through many years of cooperation with a major record label and, after his contract expired, attempted to operate a self-releasing model only to return to a major label (Hesmondhalgh and Meier 2015), are called independent artists. A concept that is used to refer to such different models should be clarified and adapted to contemporary realities, especially in the context of such a diverse phenomenon as crowdfunding.

The structure of the book reflects these aspirations. In the second chapter, we explain and organize terminology related to crowdfunding. Much has been written about this phenomenon, but not always in the context of culture and media. Even if crowdfunding platforms that organize fundraising in fields completely unrelated to culture were omitted, not every project on platforms that are closely associated with culture is cultural in character. For example, on the Kickstarter platform, whose mission is "to help bring creative projects to life," the technology category is the third largest, and though invention is a creative activity, it does not belong to the area of "culture and media." Given the quantity of publications about crowdfunding written from the perspective of finance and business studies, only those threads in this rather hermetic literature that are relevant to research of media and culture should be selected. This objective is achieved in Chapter 2. The chapter also challenges the common belief that crowdfunding is an absolute novelty and a revolutionary change. Without questioning the innovativeness of using the internet to raise money, we show that the idea of crowdfunding – a social practice that can be called "collective patronage" – has a long tradition.

Chapters 3 and 4 describe what independence in film and music is all about and analyze the place of crowdfunding in the development and distribution of cultural products, illustrating this with case studies. The structures of these chapters are similar. They begin by exploring the rich literature on independence. In both film and music, this concept has been of great importance to professionals and audiences alike – and has also been of considerable interest to researchers. Since the understanding of independence in film differs to some extent from its understanding in music, and because the issue has been analyzed separately by researchers specializing in either film or music, we devote our discussion of it to two separate chapters. Readers interested only in independence in film, for example, will not have to familiarize themselves with issues related to independence in music. After their theoretical parts, the chapters analyze how crowdfunding is used in film and music and how crowdfunding platforms operate, and cases of crowdfunding campaigns conducted in different countries are presented. Our analyses draw on multiple data sources: campaign websites, interviews conducted with artists and platform founders (available online or conducted by ourselves), and secondary sources such as industry reports.

The last part of the book summarizes these analyses and considers possibilities for the evolution of crowdfunding.

2 Crowdfunding as a new form of financing creative activity

Crowdfunding in a nutshell

Although the first internet-based crowdfunding platform, ArtistShare, was created in 2001, and the first usage of the term "crowdfunding" in internet relations dates back to 2006, the social mechanism of collecting money for predefined purposes has a long history. The practice, which may be described as "collective patronage," was used, for example, to finance the creation of operas in the 17th century (De Lucca 2011). Another, frequently cited, example of proto-crowdfunding is the Statue of Liberty. The collection of money, announced in the newspaper *New York World* in 1885, helped finance the erection of the pedestal for the Statue of Liberty. Joseph Pulitzer, one of the people behind the collection, "made a direct appeal to American patriotism and the working-class solidarity, encouraging people to respond to the gift made by the French working people" (Gómez-Diago 2015, 173). What is interesting is that the donors could count on a reward: their name and the amount donated would be placed in a special section of the above-mentioned newspaper. The applied mechanism was quite similar to present-day crowdfunding, the only difference being that the medium used to promote the collection was a newspaper. Another example of early crowdfunding are donations made by listeners to the first radio broadcasts in the early days of this medium in the 1920s (Fernández Sande and Gallego Pérez 2015). Soon after that, advertising and public money became such significant sources of financing for radio stations that today the use of proto-crowdfunding for this purpose seems a curiosity.

The breaking point in the development of crowdfunding in its present-day form was utilizing the internet in the money collection process. This helped lower the cost of collecting money, which in turn lowered the barriers to entry – arranging the collection was no longer an activity requiring large expenses. The first attempts to organize money collection with the use of the network were made without the intermediation of crowdfunding platforms – highly specialized entities creating the frames for a collection – and that is why they were similar to the practices of "collective patronage" of earlier days. The difference was that physical letters containing the request for donation were replaced with a website, email, and a mailing list. The collections arranged by the band Marillion were done in 1997 in this way, when they collected $60,000 to finance their North American tour, and in 2000, when they took paid-in-advance orders for their next album, yet to be recorded (Tuomola 2004). Mark Kelly from Marillion recalls the situation: "We emailed the 6000 fans on our database to ask, »Would you buy the album in advance?« most replied »yes.« We took over 12,000 pre-orders and went on to use the money to fund the writing and recording of the album" (Simon 2013).

The first crowdfunding platforms were created in the first decade of the 21st century. After the previously mentioned ArtistShare (founded in 2001) had been launched, others emerged – to mention just a few: Kiva (2005), Sellaband (2006), IndieGoGo (2008), and Kickstarter (2009). Interestingly, Kickstarter, which is known today as a leader in the field of creative projects, was not the first platform of this type. Apart from these platforms, there are hundreds of other entities in the world that can be classified as organizers of the crowdfunding process, and the diversity in this sector is sizable. This diversity is influenced both by the legal regulations and the strategies employed by platforms looking for a niche in specific markets.

It should be also noted that, in most cases, crowdfunding is organized by private businesses, which – as private businesses – can go bankrupt, either because of bad management or deliberate fraud. Despite being engaged in high numbers of financial transactions using other people's money, crowdfunding platforms in many countries, unlike banks, are not monitored by regulators. Although bankruptcies of crowdfunding platforms specializing in media and cultural projects occurred throughout the 2010s, their magnitude was not remarkable until the bankruptcy of Pledgemusic in 2019. Unfortunately, in this case, a large number of project initiators and contributors lost significant sums of money, estimated to be about $9.5 million in total (King 2019). We should always remember that if a platform is poorly managed or its managers engage in business malpractice – this seems to have been the case with Pledgemusic – then users of the platform, being worse informed parties, are particularly prone to exploitation.

Such bankruptcies are also harmful to other platforms as they undermine trust in the whole industry.

The global value of the crowdfunding market in May 2018 was $54.85 billion (Marketing Research 2019, 45). In Europe, it was respectively $14.89 billion (Marketing Research 2019, 48). It should be emphasized that these values include all types of crowdfunding, and creative projects constitute only a fraction.

Typology of crowdfunding and the entities participating in it

Because the literature on crowdfunding, especially in the areas of finance and entrepreneurship, is relatively extensive (see e.g. Brüntje and Gajda 2016; Landström et al. 2019; Méric et al. 2016), it is not necessary that we write broadly about business aspects of crowdfunding. However, considering that crowdfunding (in its current form) is still a relatively new phenomenon, we think that a synthetic arrangement of terminology will help readers better comprehend the further part of the text. Let us start by identifying the entities participating in crowdfunding. They are:

- Crowdfunding platforms – the entities mediating between project initiators and contributors in the process of fund collection;
- Project initiators, or requesters – the entities collecting funds, via the internet, for the implementation of their projects; and
- Backers, or contributors – people supporting the projects with their money.

Platforms

Before presenting the diverse forms of crowdfunding platforms, let us address a more general question: why they are called "platforms," and not, for instance, enterprises, undertakings, or companies? Actually, platforms take on several aspects of these organizational forms – Kickstarter, for example, is incorporated as a benefit corporation (Kickstarter 2015a). Regardless of whether they are incorporated or not, institutions organizing the process of crowdfunding are called platforms, and this word is associated with them even more than with other new-tech companies that, from an economic point of view, can also be called platforms, e.g. Facebook or Spotify.

The term "platform" has become increasingly popular during the last 15 years, to denote: online sites and services that

a) host, organize, and circulate users' shared content or social interactions for them,
b) without having produced or commissioned (the bulk of) that content,
c) built on an infrastructure, beneath that circulation of information, for processing data for customer service, advertising, and profit. (Gillespie 2018, 18)

Although the word "platform" suggests neutrality, as if all the involved parties are equal, platforms are institutions with their own interests, business models, regulations they face or attempt to avoid, and terms of use that cannot be negotiated by users. When discussing any type of platform, we should remember that this term hides certain meanings. For example, platforms that are seemingly open to everybody actively moderate the content they distribute (Gillespie 2010). The complexity of a platform's business is well explained by Prey (2020) and the example of Spotify. While the company is the leader in music streaming, it navigates uncertain waters trying to find a balance between specificities of three markets vital to its existence: the music market, the advertising market, and the financial market. Although crowdfunding platforms specializing in creative products usually deal with smaller players than Spotify (e.g. artists and individual contributors rather than labels), the multi-sided character of markets they operate on should be acknowledged. Taking all this into account, we treat crowdfunding platforms as entities that organize and govern the online process of gathering funds for multiple projects, usually for some kind of fee. There are several ways this can be done, which gives rise to classifications of types of crowdfunding platforms.

Based on how the fundraising process is shaped and what donors get in exchange for their donations, the following types of crowdfunding can be distinguished:

- Donation-based crowdfunding, where contributors cannot count on any material rewards; this form of crowdfunding applies primarily to (broadly understood) charity;
- Reward-based crowdfunding, where backers, in return for their donations, receive rewards, which usually depend on the amount of the donation; it is up to the campaign initiator to decide what the rewards are and how reward thresholds are set; in many cases, this form of crowdfunding can be understood as pre-sale;
- Lending-based crowdfunding, which involves using the internet to borrow funds from multiple investors as part of one campaign;

this form of crowdfunding is practically inapplicable to the vast majority of creative projects;
- Equity-based crowdfunding, called also crowdinvesting – "a financing method for young ventures and other commercial projects that supports the acquisition of equity by coordinating the submission of different forms of shares to an undefined group of possible investors through social virtual communities" (Hagedorn and Pinkwart 2016, 72); this form of crowdfunding is rarely applicable to the vast majority of creative projects; and
- Royalty-based crowdfunding, which "generally involves investors receiving a percentage of revenue derived from a license or a usage-based fee for the other parties' right to the ongoing use of an asset, rather than interest on a loan or appreciation in capital stock (equity)" (Massolution 2015, 43); this form of crowdfunding is therefore similar to equity crowdfunding, but it entails payment of royalties rather than ownership of an asset; as with lending-based and equity-based crowdfunding, this form of crowdfunding is rarely applicable to the vast majority of creative projects.

Another classification, one particularly important from the point of view of creative projects, is the division into platforms organizing one-time crowdfunding, and repeated patronage crowdfunding. The platforms dealing with one-time crowdfunding (e.g. Kickstarter, Indiegogo) create frameworks for running individual campaigns. If project initiators want to carry out two collections simultaneously, or one after another, they can do so, but they will be treated as two separate campaigns. Patronage crowdfunding, represented e.g. by the Patreon platform, involves contributors who make regular (usually monthly) payments to the project initiator. These payments, as in the case of single campaigns, may be in different amounts that correspond to levels set by the project initiator and give contributors various benefits. In the case of creative activities, patronage is usually aimed at providing the artists with a regular income stream, which is to help them focus on their creative work. This, of course, does not preclude the project initiator from declaring a specific purpose for a collection in a given month (or a longer period), however, the basic assumption is that subscribers are given some content on a regular basis. This crowdfunding model urges the project initiator to regularly provide contributors with benefits which, from their point of view, justify prolonging the subscription for another month.

Of course, in the case of most platforms implementing one-time crowdfunding, there are no contraindications for the project initiator to announce subsequent collections. The convergence of both models is possible through extending the offer of one-time crowdfunding platforms with subscription options characteristic of patronage crowdfunding. Kickstarter attempted this when it bought the patronage-based platform Drip in 2016 but decided to close it in November 2019.

Project initiators

Project initiators are individuals or organizations that seek financing for their projects by appealing to contributors through crowdfunding platforms. When examining the motivations of project initiators, the diversity of crowdfunding should be taken into account. While it would be a logical assumption that, in most cases, the main rationale is to collect funds, in the case of some types of projects – especially those in the area of culture and art – other motives may be equally important. According to Gerber and Hui, such an additional incentive may be, for example:

- Making the artist (project, product, etc.) more popular, which is based on the assumption that the collection, regardless of its final effect, will bring greater recognition to the person who organized it and to what that person is doing;
- Forming connections with backers, which is based on the assumption that proper communication with the users of the crowdfunding platform can help build long-term relationships with potential recipients of products made by the initiator of the collection;
- Gaining approval, which helps to determine whether people really want a product, meaning that crowdfunding becomes a form of product-testing;
- Maintaining control, which assumes that, thanks to fundraising on the crowdfunding platform, the project initiators will not have to enter into relationships that could limit their independence, e.g. relationships with business angels, entertainment corporations, etc.;
- Learning new fundraising skills, which is based on the assumption that fundraising on a crowdfunding platform requires the mastering of many communication and marketing skills, which, even in the event of a collection failure, may bring benefits to its organizer in the future (2016, 48–52); or
- Gaining community feedback, which is based on the belief that, in some cases, the community of contributors can bring unique knowledge to the project, knowledge that will be more valuable than information that can be obtained as a result of classic marketing research (Smith 2015).

As mentioned, these type of incentive complement the paramount one, which is the desire to raise funds for the implementation of one's own project. From the point of view of our discussion on independence, this motivation is essential. Crowdfunding, prescinding from its weaknesses (these will be discussed in the following chapters), is one of the few relatively easily available financing options for those artists who do not want to or cannot use traditional sources, such as publishers, music labels, grants distributed by state institutions and NGOs, or business sponsorship. At the same time, it should be emphasized that crowdfunding will not suit every artist and every type of project. First of all, running a collection is a very time-consuming and labor-intensive activity, and when an artist devotes time here, it means that he or she is not spending that time on creative activity (playing music, writing a book, working on a film). Hunter, writing about journalistic crowdfunding, summarizes this situation with one sentence: "It's like having a second full-time job" (2016, 217). Secondly,

> crowdfunding might uniquely advantage particular personality types as well as those who prior to crowdfunding already have a well-established community of supporters beyond their immediate circle of family, friends, and acquaintances, leaving out many creators who could make important cultural contributions but have neither the inclination to expose themselves to others nor an already existing community of admirers.
> (Davidson and Poor 2015, 302)

These obstacles can, to some degree, be mitigated by the choice of crowdfunding platform – some of them allow a more direct relationship with contributors, but it is still a fact that being somewhat of an extrovert helps in organizing the collection.

Contributors

Contributors are individuals who monetarily support crowdfunding projects. This rather simple definition includes a whole range of complex motivations that drive these backers. In one of the first studies on crowdfunding, Aitamurto (2011) analyzed the motivations of contributors supporting journalistic projects on the Spot.Us platform. She concluded that the main motive of contributors was their commitment to acting to promote the common good and their belief that the issues being proposed by project initiators ought to be publicized.

Some donations were made because a given matter was important to the contributor due to personal reasons (e.g. the proposed news report concerned the area where he or she was living). Aitamurto also observed that "donating seems to create a sense of connectedness" (2011, 440). These observations were confirmed by Gerber and Hui, who distinguished the following motivations that drive contributors: "Collect Rewards" (denotes a perception of crowdfunding as a form of pre-ordering), "Help Others" (altruistic motives), "Be Part of a Community" (provides a sense of belonging), and "Support a Cause" (gives an opportunity to express one's beliefs) (2013, 14–17). Similar conclusions were reached by Jian and Shin (2015, 181), who analyzed the motivations of individuals supporting journalistic projects and determined that the "belief in freedom of content, altruism, and contributing to their communities were the strongest self-reported motivations by donors of crowdfunded journalism, fun and supporting family and friends emerged as clear predictors for high levels of contributions." In the case of journalistic projects, socio-cultural motivations seem to be especially important because, from the perspective of a contributor, supporting a given project means contributing to the establishment of a given viewpoint (which, we can assume, reflects the beliefs of the contributor) within public discourse.

Galuszka and Bystrov analyzed motivations of users of the MegaTotal platform (see also Chapter 4 in this volume), which concentrated on music projects. They found that the strongest motivations related to "willingness to support artists," "willingness to listen to unknown music for free," and "willingness to buy legal (non–pirated) music," while less frequently reported motivations included "way of spending free time," "need to contact other fans," "game/form of competition," and "investment"[1] (2014, n.p.). Leibovitz et al. suggest that, in general, "personal connection between creators and backers" is an important factor for engaging in crowdfunding (2015, 19). This corresponds with observations that beginning entrepreneurs, and those who do not rely on crowdfunding, first turn to family and friends for funds (Davidson and Poor 2016). The same seems to be true for some crowdfunders, who in the beginning rely most of all on support from their immediate social circle (Davidson and Poor 2016). It is reasonable to assume that those contributors who support different projects over a long time span or, in other words, are experienced crowdfunders, have also a more diverse range of motivations than helping their friends or families. Research by Leibovitz et al. (2015) on film crowdfunding suggests that frequent backers are motivated by quality perception, offered rewards, and shared interest. This relates to more the general motivation discovered in the crowdfunding of non-creative products: "a desire to make-the-product-happen" (Zvilichovsky et al. 2018, 91).

Fans are an important group among contributors, especially in the case of cultural and entertainment projects. The motives driving fans are complex; they overlap with the motives distinguished by the authors quoted earlier in this section, and they reflect the active manner in which fans consume media products (Bennett et al. 2015). Fans may support projects on crowdfunding platforms, for example, to get "symbolically closer to production" (Hills 2015, 192) or to experience being a part of a project or a part of "an imagined community of supporters" (190). Participation in a project, even if it involves small financial contributions, may translate into obtaining access to discussions among other contributors or a possibility to interact with the artist, that is, the initiator of a project (D'Amato 2014). Fans may particularly value the fact that an artist spending a considerable amount of time on the platform is able to offer more of his or her attention than is the case for social networking sites devoid of financial aspects. In a sense, fans "buy" the attention of an artist through their contributions.

Projects carried out on reward-based platforms may give the backers an opportunity to obtain unique (i.e. impossible to buy otherwise) merchandise for higher contributions, such as special backer t-shirts, a sheet of paper with the handwritten first draft of a song, or an autograph (Thürridl and Kamleitner 2016). It should be noted that it is important for a fan to participate in the "creative process itself, not just the resultant product" (Scott 2015, 172). The effect of this participation depends, of course, on the type of the project, the nature of the fandom, and the number of fans. For some fans, the "experience of participation" itself may be enough; for others, influencing the final version of a product will be most important. In the case of large and actively involved groups of fans, the pressure on a project initiator may be so strong that the final product financed by fans will have to, at least to some degree, meet their expectations. This was the case with the film *Veronica Mars*, for instance, where the project initiator had to yield a certain degree to the expectations of fan-sponsors when creating the film (Navar-Gill 2018; Scott 2015). The possibility of having even a small impact on the final version of the financed product may be a significant motive for some fans to participate in the crowdfunding process.

What factors contribute to project success?

As is the case with other generalizations regarding crowdfunding, the answer to the question of what determines the success of a project depends on the type of crowdfunding and the rules defined by the platform. From an analytical point of view, the most appropriate approach would be to examine how the money that had been raised and how a product or event created on this basis influenced the artist's career. Such analyses are difficult because it is not always obvious which factors determined the course of the artist's career. While it is easy to see that the funds raised on a crowdfunding platform helped, for example, publish a book, at the same time it is difficult to say with certainty what other factors contributed to the final success or failure of a book financed in this way, and to the artist's career path. It might be, for example, that such a book failed to sell a large number of copies due to insufficient promotion, among other reasons. This raises the question of whether the crowdfunding campaign, which made it possible to raise funds for publishing the book but did not have regard to the need of raising additional funds to finance its promotion, was a well-planned collection. Because such dilemmas are difficult to generalize and, therefore, almost always need to be considered separately, we decided to adopt a simpler definition of "project success." By a "project success" we mean effective collection of the intended amount of money or – in the case of platforms that allow for the use of funds despite not collecting 100% of the previously set amount – obtaining the funds necessary to achieve the goal. This understanding of "project success" has been used by several researchers, whose studies show that:

- Projects whose initiators have extensive social networks and relationships have a greater chance of success (Wang 2016);
- The use of video to promote the project (embedded on the project page on the platform) increases the chances of project success (Marelli and Ordanini 2016);
- Projects that include special offers to attract contributors in the early stages of the collection have a better chance of success (Marelli and Ordanini 2016);
- Setting too long a period for a collection, too high an amount, and revealing that the project initiator has a small number of friends/likes on Facebook (fewer than 500) reduce the chances of project success (Marelli and Ordanini 2016); and
- In the case of individuals who successively implemented more than one project on the same platform, the characteristics of

payments for the first project may be a predictor of the course of subsequent collections. Project initiators with better chances of success are those whose first project was supported by a large number of contributors donating on average smaller amounts (as opposed to projects financed by a small number of contributors making large donations) and whose first project exceeded the set collection goal (i.e. more funds were collected) (Davidson and Poor, 2015).

When analyzing the success of a project, it should be noted that a significant part of the research conducted so far has been based on data collected on the Kickstarter platform and was of a quantitative nature. The inclusion of data from other platforms, especially those operating locally, as well as qualitative data might reveal additional, previously unidentified patterns. We will try to fill some of these gaps in the following chapters.

Crowdfunding and barriers to entry to cultural markets

Crowdfunding should be evaluated in the broader context of changes that occur as a result of the spread of social media and online trade in cultural products. An in-depth analysis of the changes that took place in these areas over the past 20 years would require much more space than the few paragraphs that we can devote to this topic here (the reader interested in such analysis can find it in e.g. Hesmondhalgh 2019). For this reason, we will focus solely on one aspect of these changes, the one most important for our analysis: the role of crowdfunding in removing barriers to entry into cultural markets.

By "barriers to entry," economists mean obstacles that make it difficult for new entities to appear in the market. More precisely speaking, "[a]n economic barrier to entry is a cost that must be incurred by a new entrant and that incumbents do not or have not had to incur" (McAfee et al. 2004, 463). These barriers may be, among others, in the form of legal provisions (e.g. the need to obtain a government permit to trade in a given good), cost barriers (large investments are needed to enter the market), marketing conditions (consumers are highly loyal to brands already present in the market, and it is hard to convince them to change) and specific socio-cultural circumstances (e.g. before entering the market in a given country, building social relations with future contractors may be necessary).

The emergence of crowdfunding has helped to reduce some of these barriers, but as to which barriers exactly and to what extent – this depends on the type of activity being analyzed and the specific conditions that differ from country to country. For example, a musician can use a crowdfunding platform to raise funds for an album recording, and, at the same time, she can treat the platform as a place of sale and promotion of the recording. She cannot, however, hope that the promotional activities implemented with the help of the crowdfunding platform, even if they are supported by communication through other social media, will be as effective as actions taken by a properly functioning music label. Such a label, apart from financial resources, has the required know-how and a long-established network of contacts (e.g. in traditional media) that can help the artist promote the recording. These advantages could be replaced, to a certain extent, by a combination of tools used by the artist herself, such as crowdfunding, promotion through social media, and attractive live performances, but they will not always work as well as the tools that are used with the cooperation with a record label. Of course, we should allude to two examples that combine both solutions. First, the artist, as a result of past cooperation with a music label, can already have a strong fan base that facilitates her self-promotion after she has parted with the label. This may be exemplified by the career of Amanda Palmer. Second, the artist could use the fundraising on the crowdfunding platform to sign a contract with a record label on good terms. By "good terms" we mean that he obtains a certain degree of independence from the record label on the one hand, but, on the other hand, he benefits from its know-how and network of contacts.

In the first decade of the 21st century, some researchers, prompted by optimistic visions as to the impact of the internet on the democratization of culture (e.g. Fox 2004; McLeod 2005) saw a reduction in entry barriers, for example to the music market, as a unequivocally positive phenomenon. Today it is evident that digitization, the emergence of social media, and the development of crowdfunding have had an additional consequence: an increase in cultural production. This could be interpreted as the democratization of culture – it is easier to release a recording, publish a book, or make a film – but this increase in the supply of cultural products has also had negative consequences in the form of a "buzz" that an emerging artist must break through. The number of new music albums (including premiere material) released yearly in the USA illustrates this phenomenon well. In the 1990s, there were about 30–40 thousand new releases annually; in the first decade of the 21st century, the number had doubled, reaching a peak in 2008, when 100,000 new albums were released (Lunney 2014, 292–293). It would not be so disturbing if the increase in supply was followed by an increase in demand manifested in greater spending by consumers on music. However, as Meier notes, "in 2011, roughly 2% of new releases in the United States produced 90% of new album sales" (2017, 154), which suggests that the distribution of revenue from the sale of recordings is still concentrated: a small number of top hits generate the majority of revenue. The phenomenon of an increased rivalry in the search for the attention of consumers of cultural goods has been referred to as the "dilemma of democratization" (Hracs et al. 2013, 1,148). Studying the development of crowdfunding, we cannot prescind from this phenomenon. It should be noted that a crowdfunding campaign based on cooperation with a previously established group of fans gives the project initiator a base on which he can build the promotion and distribution of a project financed in this way. This assumes that crowdfunding is treated as a method of capitalizing on a pre-existing fan base and steadily expanding it as the campaign progresses. Otherwise – in a situation where the artist treats crowdfunding as a miracle panacea for the lack of a label, without understanding that it is essential to have an audience – the collection has little chance of success. Even if it is completed, the struggle for the recipients' attention and building a sustainable career will be very challenging for individual artists.

Note

1 MegaTotal was a platform that encouraged "investing" in musical projects. This is explained in more detail in Chapter 4.

3 Crowdfunding independent cinema

On independent cinema

The academic literature on independent cinema and independence in film production is quite rich, and a detailed report of discussions of these subjects is not the purpose of this work. Such authors as Emanuel Levy, Geoff King, John Berra, and Yannis Tzioumakis have discussed these topics from different perspectives in their work.

We will focus on a few selected voices, so as to present the main themes which, in our opinion, can be developed in regard to the subject of crowdfunding. Given the need to adapt the notion of independence to the study of new forms of financing and artistic production, we will focus in particular on the dilemmas faced by film researchers who have attempted to find a common definition for diverse phenomena covering several decades, several generations, in the stylistically complex area of film production known as "independent cinema." Following in the footsteps of researchers who have addressed this problem, we treat American cinema as a starting point, because it is there that both a system of film studios and categories such as "indie" were first formed, which resulted in a certain model of film creation that attracted followers outside the United States. We assume, therefore, that it is in the United States that a certain topos of an independent filmmaker first emerged, one that is associated with a specific production model within the film industry but also influences the formation of the identity of an artist and a member of the audience and, consequently, specific cultural practices, which are the subject of our study.

In view of the above, we are aware that the conceptual apparatus we will use to study crowdfunding will need to be adapted to our case studies, which include examples from outside the United States, created under slightly different production conditions. We assume, however, that the themes we highlight in the discussion of independent cinema can be developed for and continued in recent phenomena related to community financing. This applies in particular to institutional and production issues, which, however, are closely linked to aesthetic and formal, sociopolitical, and cultural aspects in the broad sense.

Problems with the definition of independence

Independence as a category of cultural practices and creativity has been the subject of discussion and controversy for years. This applies not only to academics but also for the artists themselves, to art critics, and finally, to the audience. Independence is therefore treated as a concept used to categorize artistic creation, to value it, but also to identify it within the communities of the audience. Different levels, motivations, and areas are included in the concept. The matter at hand is not only different interpretations of what can be considered independent creation but, on a more elementary level, about agreement on the area in which the evaluation criteria should be searched for. The main focus here is on juxtaposing economic criteria, which determine artistic and cultural creativity, with aesthetic criteria that favor the dimension of an artist's expression, originality, and creativity.

This discussion particularly touches on the creative industries that are the first beneficiaries of new forms of financing such as crowdfunding, which introduces new themes but also new doubts as to what can be considered an independent production. The emergence of such opportunities, therefore, leads to a rethinking of the category of independence and its connection with the development of digital media and especially social media. Particularly noteworthy is that the new forms of financing, although they are in some respects in line with existing practices (residual economics), at the same time seem to be changing the balance of power within cultural production. On the one hand, they free artists from the influence of the giant producers, allowing artists to implement their own ideas. On the other hand, they create a stronger bond with the audience community, which willingly joins in the process of creation while expecting an opportunity to influence it. This may be contrary to the expectations of some artists, for whom freedom from a label or studio means absolute freedom and the ability to fulfill the romantic ideal of creative life. The latter remains only an ideal, because the new forms of financing require artists to provide organizational competencies that had formerly been the responsibility of the label and film studio.

The complexity of the problem is described in detail by James Bennett, who also points out that independence should be treated as:

> a rhetorical ideal that offers a utopian vision for a variety of independent media formations: impractical, unrealistic, impossible and yet, nonetheless, hopeful [...] media independence must be understood as a utopian ideal, constructed across four sites – the sociopolitical, the industrial, the formal and the rhetorical or discursive.
>
> (Bennett 2015, 1–2)

The perception of independence as utopian allows us to discuss a certain pattern that makes it possible to strive for a better model of operation by motivating and stimulating the imaginations of the audience and of artists. On the other hand, utopianism means that the achievement of the ideal of independence is actually impossible. In this situation, one can ask whether awareness of this fact is not demotivating for artists. In this context, one should perhaps speak of independence as a myth, as Daniel Kreiss does, for example in regard to Barlow's *Declaration of Independence of Cyberspace* (Kreiss 2015). However, utopia also has a mobilizing character, because it indicates deficiencies in the current model:

> media independence often functions as an argument and a call to action, to create space for new, diverse and divergent voices within a given media system.
>
> (Bennett 2015, 8)

We consider this particularly important in the case of crowdfunding, where the success of the "call for action" is based on a vision shared by the artist and a community of founders grounded in a shared understanding of independence. What is important is that different visions of independence are deeply rooted in the current sociopolitical context, which points to a specific discourse of power within which this independence is to be achieved. This affects important legal and organizational regulations, whose operation, but also contestation, affect the continuous negotiation of the understanding of independence.

This process is more pronounced today as a result of the development of various media, especially social media. Bennett writes:

> The dynamic and mutable nature of media independence is, perhaps, most apparent in the way the "New Economy" of the

creative industries has increasingly embraced different notions of independence in the move toward outsourcing, freelance and precarious labor. Here, to be independent within the media is to derive autonomy, creative freedom and choice in one's work in exchange for risk, flexibility and self-exploitation.

(Bennet, 2)

One should keep in mind, however, that the understanding of this autonomy is closely connected with the cultural myth of an independent artist. As Hesmondhalgh observes:

> creative autonomy from commercial restraint is a theme which has often been used to mystify artistic production by making the isolated genius the hero of cultural myth.
>
> (Hesmondhalgh 1999, 35)

This problem is finding its new media exposure with the development of such forms as crowdfunding, which seem to favor a low-budget aesthetic and DIY creativity. According to Bennett, this places independent art in a somewhat paradoxical situation wherein:

> On the one hand, authenticity can signify artistic value – often associated with cultural elites […] and on the other, it can connote a connection to working-class cultures that are simultaneously devalued as sites of popular, mass entertainment consumption, at the same time as they are venerated as embodiments of preindustrial folk culture. (2015, 22)

This echoes recurring dilemmas and discussions about popular and mass culture (cultural studies) and, in the understanding of Pierre Bourdieu, "taste distinctions." In this context, it is important for us not to consider independence only from the perspective of taste or as a system of production (power and control). The perspective proposed by James Bennett is therefore useful. He distinguishes four fields in which the problem of independence can be considered: the industrial, the formal, the sociopolitical, and the rhetorical. The most interesting for our study is the rhetorical, which:

> operates across the other three sites and is mobilized by producers, audiences, regulators, businesses and a range of vested interests in declaring this or that formation to be "independent media." It is here we find media independence most often expressed as a

utopian ideal within which a particular "independent media" might operate. (4)

What is important, according to the Bennett, is that such a complex structure makes it possible to see independent music as the best example of independence in media. In our opinion, independent cinema shares the above characteristics, especially when we consider such issues as autonomy in the context of the production system or relying on the myth of an independent artist (whether musician or director). An additional difficulty in defining independence in the areas of film and music, however, is that independent media have much in common with alternative media, especially in terms of their objectives and aesthetics. This problem in defining the concept of independence leads, as Bennett points out, to the following consequence:

> [because of] their refusal to occupy the margins of radically alternative media – independent media are in a nearly perpetual state of crises. (19)

These crises are varied in nature: economic, which is associated with financing problems; ethical, associated with the opinion of the public about sources of financing; and formal, associated with the unique characteristics of cultural production and the audience for which its products are intended. Regarding film – a specific cultural production – Geoff King also indicates its continuous functioning "simultaneously in crisis and renewal," although "the two positions are mutually implicated rather than simply opposed" (2013, 45).

We can therefore say that media are independent in a constant cycle of change and transformation – from a contestational ideal to a pragmatic compromise. The term "hybridity" proposed by Bennett is particularly useful at this point to describe the complex systemic relationships within which media carry out the narratives of independence (9), which, in our opinion, are particularly relevant to crowdfunding. These relationships enter into completely new forms, especially in the case of the relationship between creativity and commerce (Hesmondhalgh 1999, 35). It can be said that we are dealing with the emergence of completely new forms of autonomy which coexist with the existing system of creative industries:

> The basic structural characteristics of creative industries – their technologies of production and consumption – fiercely resist governance by anything approaching a complete contrast. Yet they have

evolved distinctive and serviceable contract forms that seem to differ from deal-making patterns prevalent in other sectors.

(Caves 2003, 73)

When considering these problems, however, one should bear in mind the unique characteristics of cultural products – which include film and music. The status of independence in both types of production is related to the aforementioned myth of an artist and the issue of the proposed autonomy. However, with regard to Caves's remarks:

> In order for all the opportunities, particularly those of an economic nature, to be realized, compromises with regard to the autonomy of the artist, or director, may have to be enforced and endured.
>
> (Berra 2008, 10)

According to Berra, this reduces independent cinema to a "field of cultural production within the field of power" (Berra 2008, 14). However, to return to Bennett's concept, we believe that in this case as well:

> Analyzing independence across these four sites in relation to any media system, however, produces a complex, and at times contradictory, understanding of the concept that demonstrates how different actors within a given media system enlist independence rhetorically and discursively to meet particular ideals. (5)

We consider it crucial to understand independence as a utopian ideal that functions as a "motivating factor and discursive structure that influences media systems, and the individuals who work within them, around the globe" (10). Film production would appear to be an especially interesting example of the operation of this function.

When considering independence in cinema, it is important to point out its extremely problematic nature, which manifests itself at levels ranging from the fact that there is no consensus as to the temporal scope of the phenomena it is supposed to cover, to the fact that shifting the considerations toward both aesthetic (style) and economic (production system) issues is debatable. In this context, John Berra points out that this topic is "academically non-established" for the following reasons:

> Firstly, a rigid definition of American "independent" cinema is hard to pinpoint. Secondly, the term has only gained cultural significance since the early 1990s, meaning that its place in the

popular consciousness is still in a formative state. Thirdly, it is arguable that American "independent" cinema is still not finite, existing somewhere between being a form of technical production, and the idealized conceptual model for any auteur wishing to use film as their form of popular expression. (11)

This leads to a situation where it becomes difficult to treat "independence" as a purely productive category – as was initially the case – because its cultural significance strongly indicates the unique characteristics of artistic expression as it unambiguously indicates certain perceptive expectations in terms of artistic style and expression. Moreover, the above issues do not exhaust the range of possibilities of defining independence in the film industry, which, combined with Bennett's categorization discussed above, makes up a set of dilemmas that will also accompany us in our study of film crowdfunding.

As John Berra and Yannis Tzioumakis write, the picture of independent cinema consists of:

> gritty location shooting with an avant-garde approach, and little-known actors. Upon completion, the results of the labours of love of such cinematic crusaders are screened in decaying art house cinemas to an audience comprised of hip urban dwellers, whose interest in low-budget feature films effectively finances an underground "movement," enabling independent film-makers to make more features in similarly economically stringent, but creatively autonomous, circumstances.
>
> (Berra 2008, 16)

and

> independence in American cinema had become associated with intelligent, meaningful, often challenging but always full of spirit filmmaking, while production by the majors was associated with conservative, conventional, formulaic and spiritually empty efforts at entertaining an increasingly young audience.
>
> (Tzioumakis 2006, 13)

Apart from the debatability of the determinants used here, which hardly meet the requirements of scientific categorization (e.g. how to determine whether a film is "full of spirit"), Tzioumakis further notes that such a stereotypical approach allows simultaneous use of the category of independence as the main element of the marketing strategy of particular films. In other words, independence in the film industry understood in this way is also a "marketing category," which seems particularly important for the issues discussed in this book – crowdfunding may also be treated as a specific marketing and measurement tool. However, defining independence from this perspective may certainly raise objections, as independent creativity is commonly associated with activities that are not primarily aimed at profit and commercial success. We will return to the issue of promotion and distribution later. Let us now look at another understanding of independence in film studies.

The oft-quoted definition of independence in this context is that suggested by Emanuel Levy:

> ideally, an indie is a fresh, low-budget movie with a gritty style and offbeat matter that express the filmmaker's personal vision.
>
> (Levy 1999, 2)

This definition includes several of the aspects mentioned above. First, the determinants of independence are to be production constraints, linked to a small budget, which by default links this type of production to smaller production entities. Films of this type are also supposed to have a particular style and, what is more, this style should be connected with the idea of art cinema, which is supposed to present an individual vision and formal distinctions. At this point it can also be added that uniqueness of style is often determined by the budget, an example of which is Kevin Smith's cult film *Clerks* (Giannetti 1999, 169), which to a large extent influences the general recognition of a certain type of cinema as independent and also determines certain audience practices. Finally, Levy's definition assumes that a determinant of independent cinema is the taking up of topics that for some reason have not found a place in mainstream cinema. This would mean issues that are both morally controversial and difficult but socially important, as well as an unconventional approach to themes and characters.

At this point, we must agree with Tzioumakis (2006) that Levy's definition does not fulfill its function at all. On the contrary, it creates even more confusion, leading to the exclusion of many works that are generally considered independent, as well as to the inclusion of productions whose independence is debatable. First, we should ask just what the artists in question are independent of. When we look back over the history of film, we see completely different understandings of this concept and different needs associated with independence.

Moreover, the enumerating nature of this definition makes it unsatisfactory in most cases. Taking it as a starting point, however, we want to look at the individual elements it lists, so as to select those aspects that will be useful for the study of crowdfunded cinema.

Position in history

Although, as Tzioumakis (2006) shows, the origins of film independence can be traced back to the beginnings of cinema, there is no doubt that the 1980s and 1990s were particularly important for independent cinema. These decades saw the works of such directors as Hal Hartley, the Coen brothers, and Jim Jarmusch, and, at the very end Steven Soderbergh, as well as the creation of a unique film culture. One should recall the pioneering artists of the late 1970s, such as David Lynch with his *Eraserhead* (1977) and John Waters with *Pink Flamingos* (1972). For this reason, Levy suggests that independent cinema should be dated starting from 1977, although he himself admits that he is forced to refer to earlier films as well (Levy 1999). John Berra dates independent cinema from 1969, regarding Ken Loach's *Kes* (1969) and Dennis Hopper's *Easy Rider* (1969) as crucial films (Berra 2008). By preferring instead the 1980s and 1990s, we emphasize that at that time a foundation was built consisting of festivals and specialized branches of majors that focused on niche film production. Moreover, important films appeared in these decades that are considered exemplary for understanding of this type of art today and, at the same time, were groundbreaking in changing the image of this type of cinema and its popularization (including *sex, lies, and videotape* (1989) by Steven Soderbergh; *Reservoir Dogs* (1992) and *Pulp Fiction* (1994) by Quentin Tarantino; and *Clerks* (1994) by Kevin Smith). As a result, changes also occurred in the area of distribution, with the development of multiplexes and the broadening of the films offered (Berra 184). As King (2005, 20–22) points out, this was also a time of searching on the part of the audience, which was tired of Hollywood's conservatism, with increased competition from video and cable distribution. The success of such films as *Reservoir Dogs* and s*ex, lies, and videotape* led to a change in the situation and a paradoxical rapprochement between independent production and Hollywood. This is because the expectations of the independent film industry had changed:

> favouring those capable of making a quick impression over those dependent on slow-burning recognition.
>
> (King 2005, 34)

As a result, the 1990s saw an increase in the production of independent films that fought for the same audience, and producers increasingly adopted a "hit" strategy. It also became increasingly difficult to define independent entities. Hence, for example, the introduction of names such as mini-majors or semi-indie for Miramax (Tzioumakis 2006, 4), which, as Alisa Perren suggests, is basically considered not so much a pioneering distributor of "edgy, low-budget, 'quality' American films" as an initiator of the internal transformation of Hollywood and the majors (Perren 2012, 3). As Levy summed up in 1999:

> Indies now form an industry that runs not so much against Hollywood as parallel to Hollywood. American culture has two legitimate film industries, mainstream and independent, each grounded in its own organizational structure. While audiences overlap for some Hollywood and indie fare, the core audience for each type of film is different too. (501)

Even when looking at such iconic phenomena as the Sundance Festival, the problem of an unambiguous definition of production becomes evident, especially when considering the problem of distribution, which we will discuss in the next section. Looking at the formal features and topics of the Sundance Festival, the problem of the "independence" of cinema seen in this context cannot be reduced to production alone. We should mention, on the one hand, the pioneering trends of the 1970s (e.g. inspirations, still present, from the French New Wave in New American Cinema, but also exploitation cinema in contemporary productions) and, on the other hand, the diverse and often ambiguous, in terms of their independence, works of directors who began their careers in the 1990s (such as Richard Linklater and Noah Baumbach) and the 2000s (such artists as the Duplass brothers and development of the *mumblecore* subgenre). This ambiguity results from, among other things, the simplistic approach to independent cinema as a simple opposite of Hollywood's "commercial" cinema, which, by definition, would be devoid of artistic value and any possibility of implementing the artist's vision. Of course, this problem is more deeply rooted and results from the aforementioned problems with the very category of independence, associated with the understanding of the role and position of an artist, as well as with a broader context of criticism of "commercial" popular and mass culture.

Looking for an analogy to the present day, one should consider whether crowdfunded cinema is not created under conditions of fatigue with the banality of high-budget productions, with a simultaneous increase in the competitiveness of VOD platforms and the transition of ambitious artists to the production of television series, which, due to the nature of their production and distribution process, allow for some risk, especially with regard to scripts. Paradoxically, this fatigue could also concern independent cinema itself, which in a certain way – especially after *sex, lies, and videotape* – became a victim of its own success. As Levy writes:

> The switch in indie philosophy has brought "corporate worries – fear of embarrassing public relations and boycotts by intolerant activists." Some fear that this new environment will lead to a chilling of the creative environment associated with indie filmmaking. (504)

In this context, as we seek to demonstrate, crowdfunded cinema creates new opportunities, based on the image of independent filmmaking created in the 1980s and 1990s but using its own promotional potential (developed especially by majors and their "independent" extensions) and perhaps affording an opportunity to refresh this "creative environment" under the conditions of the new media reality.

The myth of an independent filmmaker and Auteur style

The "filmmaker's vision" component in Levy's definition is connected with the historically clearly situated myth of an independent filmmaker. The iconic figure here is certainly John Cassavetes,

> whose approach to filmmaking created the very powerful and romantic ideology of the lone and uncompromised filmmaker who works with a dedicated circle of friends and who goes to great lengths to see his distinct vision on the screen.
>
> (Tzioumakis 2006, 174)

The precursor characters of Cassavetes, John Mekas, and Maya Deren, contributed to the creation in the 1990s of the myth and dream of becoming an independent filmmaker. It is worth noting, as King (2005, 25) and Berra (2008, 109 et seq.) do, that for many people independent cinema was treated as an element in a career path model that eventually led to Hollywood – this needs to be mentioned here, as this theme will also be present in our study of crowdfunding, which for debuting filmmakers may be akin to a platform for promotion.

The consequence of the myth is the frequent identification of independent cinema with auteur cinema as it was understood by French critics of the 1950s, which not only creates problems – taking into account the artistic path of some artists, such as Richard Linklater, whose experimental *Slacker* has not been fully reflected in his later work (e.g. *School of Rock*) – but also makes it difficult to classify mainstream filmmakers such as David Fincher, who clearly fit into the Hollywood model of film production but do not give up their artistic style or controversy. As John Berra notes in regard to a definition built on authorship:

> such a definition is blind to the economic structure of the industry, which requires directors seeking finance for projects of a certain scale and scope to work within the studio system. (76)

Moreover, as shown by artists such as Spike Lee, connections with large studios on further levels of production or distribution need not negate the artist's vision, the possibility of exploring a controversial topic, or a distinctive style.

When describing independent cinema in the context of artists, it is impossible not to mention the category of generation, sometimes used in the analysis of the phenomena already discussed. On the one hand, there is a common denominator for artists who began their artistic career at the Sundance Festival in the 1990s and 2000s, especially after the famous success of Steven Soderbergh; they are often described as the "Sundance generation" (Pitrus 2010). On the other hand, there is a special predisposition for this type of work, which can be associated with the unique characteristics of Generation X as reflected in the work of directors such as Kevin Smith, Richard Linklater, and Zack Braff (who later became one of the pioneers of crowdfunding large film projects, which we will discuss later). These filmmakers began their careers with relatively small budget projects, often carried out with the help of friends who had a clear impact on the style of their films. Technical shortcomings and amusing dialogues became the hallmark of the cinema of Generation X, and one of its distinguishing features was the pursuit of creative life at the expense of status and money. Importantly, limited distribution success was secondary to individual influence for artists such as Linklater and their creation of the cultural image of the "slacker" generation (Pierson 1997, 194). This fits the unique myth of a filmmaker:

> At the production end, especially, independent filmmaking can be intensely personal activity, less subject to the vagaries of the

commercial marketplace. Conditions of the relative financial difficulty might even be a spur to higher quality, increasing the extent to which the pictures that survive into production are those in which higher levels of creative passion are invested.

(King 2005, 51)

In this approach, raising money to finance production becomes an element of the creative process, although this is not necessarily made clear by the filmmakers themselves, who make low budgets not only an advantage but even something to be proud of (exceptionally, it may be inscribed in the ideology of Generation X with its social and professional position).

Although this relationship is elaborated by researchers such as Giannetti (1999), it is worth noting, following Pierson (228 ff.) and King, the mythology of this relationship and the size of "small" budgets in general, as

tales of feature-length movies being made on tiny budgets, shot in spare time, financed on credit cards or through funds scrambled together from other unlikely resources.

(King 2005, 12)

should be considered myths built on understatements, for example about giving up one's wages, but above all on the perception of the entire process in isolation from post-production and distribution, the cost of which often many times exceeds the cost producing an independent film – as King states in the case of *Clerks:*

completion costs totalled $200,000 with another $1.7 million spent by the distributor Miramax on print, radio and television advertising during the six-month theatrical run. (2005, 15).

This ambiguity fits perfectly Generation X, whose voice is Kevin Smith, an artist who not only does not hide his desire to move to high-budget productions (Pierson 1997) but also openly criticizes the use of crowdfunding by well-known artists and suggests that crowdfunding should be a tool for "real indie filmmakers" (McNelly 2013).

Generation X, closely linked to independent cinema in the 1990s, itself presents an ambivalent attitude towards commercialism, dissociating itself from its parents' "hippie" ideals while glorifying the consumer pleasures associated with commercial yet independent productions such as *Star Wars*. It is worth mentioning that it was the baby boomers who in the 1960s contributed to the flourishing of independent cinema, in search of topics that went beyond moral norms to touch upon political problems while at the same time breaking Hollywood conventions, where artists such as Cassavetes gained the status of heroes. As far as their children are concerned, independence as a quality of an artist still has these traits, as can be seen in both Smith's and Linklater's works (Pierson 1997), but it is not devoid of ambiguity and even cynical irony.[1]

However, the cinema of Generation X also includes David Fincher's famous *Fight Club* produced by 20th Century Fox, based on the novel by Chuck Palahniuk, which reflects the mood of resignation of Generation X and was part of the current ironic criticism of consumer culture. That said, this film can in no way be called independent, especially considering the controversies associated with the studio's limitation of Fincher's ideas (censorship of dialogue, using traditional film posters with actors' faces instead of posters with images of soap, etc.). 20th Century Fox's interference and a cast filled with movie stars, on the one hand, eliminate any possibility of linking this film in any way to the category of independent film, but, on the other, offer an interesting example of how the majors capture the strategy of independent cinema. As King rightly points out, when comparing such productions as *Lord of the Rings* and *American Beauty*, one can doubt which is actually closer to the idea of an independent film production – of course, when only type of production and topics are discussed (King 2005, 47).

Topics in independent cinema

Returning to Levy's definition of independent cinema, let us now focus on the problem of film topic. Levy's approach would oblige cinema considered to be independent to deal with difficult and socially important issues. However, this would exclude any existence of independent entertainment cinema,[2] making it virtually impossible. The question is, what should we do with, for example, the productions of Troma Studios, which are characterized by the absurdity and shallowness of their topics and by "bad taste." It is hard to deny their uniqueness of style, which has been recognizable among fans for years, and they certainly are independent with regard to financing. Moreover, since the 1960s, mainstream cinema has been moving to capture this aspect of independent cinema, thus expanding what it offers and entering into some, though often superficial, global discussions on socially important issues (e.g. the problem of the death penalty after

Tim Robbins's *Dead Man Walking*). This mainstream capture has become especially important in the era of social media, where the audience perceives many problems as elements of certain conglomerates that include fashion and lifestyle. Contemporary examples include the introduction of LGBT themes and the rights of African Americans and women into the *Avengers*. It is worth remembering, however, that this is not only connected with the discussion on the current situation of women (especially in Hollywood – #MeToo) and the desire to take up a disputable topic but also with the competition with the series based on DC Comics, which earlier, with perhaps a surprising success, used the potential of the female character Wonder Woman. The film *Black Panther* was hailed as the first film of the monumental *Avengers* series that was attractive to African-American audiences, a result of both the uniqueness of the subject and characters as well as the historical references to the Black Panthers movement. In this spirit, another interesting example is provided by Warner Bros's latest production of *Shaft*, which refers directly to cult blacksploitation cinema and one of its most famous characters. The director of the film is Tom Story, known for his typically entertaining cinema and television films, but the main role is played by Samuel L. Jackson, whose status, if one takes into account his links to independent cinema, is quite ambiguous. On the one hand, he has played in blockbuster megaproductions, but on the other, he has worked with directors such as Spike Lee and Quentin Tarantino. *Shaft*, as a production, addresses political topics and nostalgia for another time, in this case for the 1970s.

Despite this tendency for mainstream cinema to capture "independent" topics, as King notes, independent cinema is still recognizable in terms of its identity, not least because of the topics it addresses, but also because of the way in which they are presented. What is unique about them is that the audience is put in a state of discomfort resulting from the ambiguous presentation of certain topics, even if they are already recognizable in mainstream productions, an example of which is the subject of pedophilia in Todd Solondz's *Happiness* (1998). A distinguishing feature of independent cinema is, therefore, its avoidance of stereotypical representations and of the "ideologically loaded imaginary reconciliations used in Hollywood" (King 2005, 198–199). As Levy notes:

> Occasionally, there are thematic similarities between the two industries, although indies often play the upper hand. (501)

Again, controversial and socially important topics are becoming increasingly present in mainstream productions as a result of the increasingly strong presence of these topics in public discourse, especially in social media. This also leads to difficulty in assessing the use of these topics by independent cinema, because, as King notes:

> Whether independent production [...] more than occasionally constitutes a radical cinema in an explicitly political sense, rather than in the implications of a broader treatment of particular social issues, is more questionable.
>
> (King 2005, 199)

One should keep in mind that controversy as a distinguishing feature of independent cinema also attracts a specific audience, or even, as shown by Miramax's productions, may be an element of marketing strategy.

Distribution and promotion

To consider the issue of attraction, let us return to the indie category. While in the case of music we can talk about a continuum, with one end marked by media products prepared in their entirety by corporations (e.g. boy bands) and the other by radical DIY projects (e.g. the activities of the band Crass), in the case of cinema the situation is slightly different. When talking about cinema, one should bear in mind the bridge between independent cinema and Hollywood and the creation of "Indiewood" (Tzioumakis 2005, 2009).

The key here, however, is to break dominant conventions, which may often be linked to the category of generation in the sense that these contraventions are addressed to rebellious young people:

> What becomes especially important with this category of independent filmmaking is not so much the fact that film production was arranged by companies other than the major studios [...], but that a large number of independent producers consciously assaulted the codes and conventions of mainstream American filmmaking [.]
>
> (Tzioumakis 2006, 178)

What is important is that neither a small budget nor being outside the majors' system guarantees a breaking of such standards, nor do they guarantee the "independent" quality of a production, as exemplified by the activity of Carolco Pictures (King 2005, 5). This breaking of conventions does not have to mean high artistic quality, nor does it even mean choosing a minority or "art-house audience" as a target; instead, it may take the form of a controversy attractive to younger audiences. As King notes, the need to make such a choice of target and the tension between artists and distributors are unique characteristics of independent cinema (30–32). This tension seems linked in a peculiar way with the topos of an artist. Independence, on the one hand, depends on the act of transferring the distribution of independently produced films to other companies, often associated with larger studios, or on making independent distribution efforts. The latter may be related to the aforementioned romantic figure of a director, of which Cassavetes is the model, although this has its consequences as, according to Pierson (1997, 10):

> Ironically, Cassavetes' iron control of his own rights provides a crucial explanation for his waning influence of filmmakers in more recent times. The films were simply hard to see before and after his death. Theatrical exhibition consisted of the very occasional career retrospectives at places like the 1989 Sundance Film Festival.

On the other hand, many expressive artists associated with a rather radical cinema, such as Spike Lee, agree to transfer distribution to majors, separating creative process from distribution. Criticism of such an approach is often based on the erroneous separation of "independent" production from the general principles of cultural production in general, including the question of what happens to the text after it has been produced. The mythology of small film budgets is accompanied by a lack of awareness of promotion and distribution processes. These areas often require higher budgets than the production itself. This may lead to the conclusion that in the case of film production, it is difficult to speak of independence:

> The position of these "independent" film-makers within the field of power means that the term "independent" is a misleading one. No film-maker or producer is truly "independent," in that they cannot exist separately from the field of economic power, in this case represented by studios, distributors, exhibitors, and promotional media. While a creative autonomy may be achieved through self-financing, the need for art to connect to an audience entails that the film-maker is always in a compromised position.
>
> (Berra, 2008, 15)

Furthermore, self-financing is not only connected with the risk of lower availability but also with the need for new competencies, as a result of which the entire process of creation, fundraising, and distribution becomes creative work. Consequently, in practice few artists decide to undertake such risky action:

> Modern cinema has thrown up a number of examples of films that have been truly independent in terms of financing, but the financial demands placed upon any individual who tries to promote and distribute their finished feature are so great that, at this stage, it is often necessary for a larger film company to step in.
>
> (Berra 2008, 77)

This problem seems particularly important in the context of crowdfunding. However, we perceive the situation of crowdfunded cinema as different due to the development of social media and the strengthened visibility of texts and artists located in the "long tail" (Anderson 2006). This allows perhaps a more optimistic view than that suggested by Berra of the position of an independent artist who, despite giving up the participation of large studios in promotion and distribution, is no longer doomed to having only a cinephile set audience (106). Film crowdfunding may make it possible to bridge the "gap" identified by Berra:

> Distribution within the independent sector suffers because it is rarely the case that the creative and financial team that put together a film is actually involved in releasing it, leading to a gap between completion and distribution. (2008)

However, this assumption certainly does not eliminate the problem. Also important from this perspective is determining the position of independent cinema in a context built by critics and the festival base. In the absence of a budget for traditional advertising, these create opportunities for a gradual introduction of the film (e.g. "platform release" (King 2005, 26; Berra 2008, 80)) and for establishing contacts with distributors after the initial introduction of the film on small screens and at festivals and, as a result, separating production from distribution. Looking for an equivalent of this strategy is interesting from the standpoint of crowdfunding with its exclusive access to certain content during a campaign and the gradual increase of activities throughout its development. As far as independent cinema is concerned, the key precursor is Daniel Myrick and Eduardo Sánchez's

Blair Witch Project (1999), which was the first film to make full use of the possibilities of the word-of-mouth strategy, which in the case of crowdfunded cinema will become a necessity and a basis for building the success of a campaign.

Conclusion

In summing up this part of the book, we outline the conceptual framework that will be used to study crowdfunding. As far as inspirations from the area of independent cinema studies are concerned, the most useful are the proposals of Geoff King, Yannis Tzioumakis, and John Berra. We, therefore, assume, as does King (2005), that various film productions financed through crowdfunding can be included in a system defined by three determinants. The first is the place in the production system, which includes such aspects as the degree of "independence" – independent distribution, or maintaining such independence only at the production stage; the position of the artist (artists with an established position or debutants); and the area that is financed by crowdfunding (using crowdfunding as a subsidy for certain parts of the film budget or as a tool for marketing and market research). The second regards aesthetic and formal issues, which, however, we want to examine first and foremost in connection with the film budget. The third and final determinant refers to the broader cultural context and political and ideological issues, or the tendency of independent productions to address difficult and controversial topics, albeit ones that are socially desirable. Following in the footsteps of John Berra, we see independence as:

> a method of production and a form of cultural expression, worthy of analysis within a social-political context. (12)

The proposal of James Bennett, with his division into four fields describing independence (with the rhetorical field occupying the key position) and his treatment of independence in accordance with an idealistic understanding of it as a "motivating factor and discursive structure," is also useful in this context.

We believe that crowdfunding should be analyzed in such a context because of its location in the broader perspective of technological and social transformation. John Berra points to differences in the sequence of actions within mainstream cinema and in cinema that can be considered independent. One such difference is that in the latter production starts with an original screenplay text, while in films produced by large studios the script is written and the film crew is assembled only after it has been determined that the project is likely to be profitable (Berra 2008, 20). Crowdfunding introduces further changes in this area and starts the process from building a fanbase and an audience that knows exactly what to expect in terms of the content and the people associated with the project. This makes it necessarily more sensitive to the moods and needs of the audience regarding topic. The example of the Polish documentary *Just Don't Tell Anyone*, discussed later, shows the extent to which this type of production also allows for the active political involvement of the audience, which significantly changes film production by refreshing the concept of independence and placing it firmly in a social and political context.

Taking the three aspects proposed by King into account will enable us to provide various examples that more or less meet the requirements for independence set out above. Bearing in mind the various areas of operation of the concept of independence, we want to emphasize productive and technological aspects, accepting, as does King (2005, 2), the fact that any breach of standards, on either the artistic or the ideological level, must be linked to a certain distance and freedom from the constraints imposed by the dominant system of production.

We also want to take into account the suggestion that the category of independence, as the basis for a certain discourse, is historically conditioned. In other words, it requires asking each time the following question about a specific author and work: what exactly are they independent from? Following the history of American cinema, one can see fascinating transformations and blurring of boundaries, which, without this assumption, would render the category of independence almost useless. In the case of crowdfunded cinema, this question grows even more interesting, as it includes a new entity – fanvestors – in the discussion and places social and technological transformations in the foreground. This inclusion requires a redefinition of both the position of the author and any analysis of the degree and manner in which the topos of an independent artist, and the romantic myth of a film director as an auteur, are used. The myth may serve as a marketing technique to consolidate fanvestors around the image of a personal brand (a kind of tribal marketing built on the myth of independence), but it may also constitute a barrier from the standpoint of authors who perceive crowdfunding as a tool for absolute independence but do not notice the unique characteristics of this reversed production mechanism and their dependence on the financing community. This problem should be considered from the perspective of the recognition of independence as both "motivating factor and discursive structure."

This takes us to Tzioumakis's approach to independence as discourse, as understood by Michel Foucault. The discourse imposed by social media and participatory culture (Jenkins 2006) introduces a shift in power among the entities creating the language of the discourse of independence. It is crucial to link technological change with the wider dimension of social change and the complexity of their mutual relationship. In the past, the technological aspect itself also had a significant impact on independent productions, manifested in the availability of cheap video equipment that significantly lowered production costs and facilitated the access of debutants (expressed, for example, in the absence of the need to obtain permission to film) or through digital projection capabilities, which facilitated the presentation of the final work to distributors and even facilitated distribution in small, independent venues (King 2005, 51–55). These transformations influenced the overall understanding of independence formed within the discourse created by studios, artists, critics, and audiences. They also affected marketing techniques, which have used and continue to use the concept of independence as a lure for a specific target consumer. As Berra writes:

> It is now necessary to look at the technological changes, and market needs that have made some form of "independent" production possible today, and enhanced Hollywood's interest in, and accommodation of, that cinema, while also observing how the strategies of the corporate giants make it possible for such "subtle forms of intervention" to creep into the culture of mass consumption. (19)

Interestingly, King compares these changes to music production, where MP3s and network distribution capabilities were a breakthrough (54). Again, a particularly important example of the impact of technological development is the *Blair Witch Project*, as a pioneering film in terms of the use of the internet for marketing and building a fanbase before the actual distribution of the otherwise unknown film. This is becoming the norm in the case of crowdfunded cinema but also for crowdfunded music.

Finally, we would like to point out that the shift is happening in the understanding of the creative process itself, which, as King (2005, 13) suggests, includes fundraising, which can be as creative as creating a film itself. In crowdfunding, this process is included in the community context understood as co-creation, in which the audience becomes actual co-authors of the film within the framework of participatory culture (Jenkins 2006). This is a further development of strategies used by artists such as Spike Lee and Troma but with a significant shift towards a more or less anonymous and completely uncontrollable "crowd."

It is therefore important to look at independence from the standpoint of audience strategies (Newman 2012). In the case of crowdfunding, these penetrate deep into the process of creation of a text, inextricably intertwining it with the financing process as a creative process. It is necessary to take into account the problem of participatory culture and the context of fandom studies which, in the form suggested by Henry Jenkins, can better describe the audience of independent crowdfunded cinema than the above-mentioned and hitherto used categories of "arthouse audience" and "cinephile set." Returning to the question of "taste," we assume that the division into "popular audience" and audiences "seeking works of higher social value," as in Pierre Bourdieu's writings, is unsustainable in the current media reality, although consideration should also be given to John Berra's comment that:

> It should be noted, however, that this crossover in audience interest does not occur immediately, and it is the cinephile set, or at least those more discerning audience members, who are relied on to show initial "support" to an independent feature and spread favourable word of mouth. (182)

One must keep in mind that in participatory culture the conditions for creating discourse are completely changed, and the role of entities such as professional film critics is marginalized. The new conditions are also changing the determinants of marketing, which is becoming human-centric (Kotler et al. 2016), favoring forms that were of key importance to independent cinema in the past such as word-of-mouth (Berra 2008, 163), but in their new version are present in social media.

The border between a "top" independent production and a Hollywood one is becoming increasingly blurred, but this does not mean, as King (2005, 16) notes, that there is no room for "innovative and low-cost indie filmmaking." In our opinion, this place can be successfully filled by a production financed by crowdfunding, which, without abandoning some of these systemic ambiguities, introduces new aspects of independence that were previously absent or only outlined in filmmaking.

Crowdfunded independent cinema

Introduction

In this section, we present examples of crowdfunding campaigns that demonstrate the various faces of independent film and ways of approaching this new formula of financing. We will draw attention to the determinants of independence in the film industry described in the previous section. First and foremost, our area of interest is placement in the production system – in others words the position of the artist therein. An example is provided by Zach Braff as an artist with a fairly stable position in indie mini majors cinema, but who is also associated with mainstream film and television production. Troma is in a completely different situation, functioning since the beginning of its existence as an independent production and distribution company but associated with a very niche type of B-class cinema directed not so much to a "cinephile" audience as its fans. Troma is interesting if we consider the question of area, which is financed by crowdfunding. Hence, we will be interested in the use of crowdfunding as a subsidizing of only certain aspects of production or as a tool for marketing and market analysis, since this approach is proposed by the president of the Troma company. A significant role here is played by another of the factors described in the previous chapter, specifically the linking of the film form with budget. In the case of Troma, the form is of necessity related to budget, while at the same time it becomes an aesthetic distinction that bonds the fan community. It should be emphasized here that the specificity of the genre of horror ("the forgiving genre") allows for it. The fan audience of this genre not only forgives creators for technical shortcomings caused by budget shortages but even derives pleasure from these shortcomings, because they introduce a comical element, making the experience more complex (Church 2010).

In turn, the issues of cultural, social, and political-ideological context can be clearly seen in the example of Zach Braff as a "generational" director who attempts to show an unconventional approach to traditional social systems. A second instance is provided by the Polish example of the Sekielski brothers' film, which touches upon extremely sensitive social and political-ideological issues, so that its implementation outside the official financing system also becomes a kind of political manifesto. Here appear the issues of discussion over what a socially desired subject is. This discussion gains a completely new dimension when we consider the specifics of the Patronite platform.

Crowdfunding, due to a peculiar reversal of the order of film production, begins the whole process by building a fanbase as a certain community, which makes it more sensitive to the moods and needs of an audience interested in specific problems. We see manifestations of this phenomenon in both aforementioned examples – one intended as a generational manifesto and the other addressing the problem of pedophilia among Polish priests, a problem that divides society.

We also want to place emphasis on the production aspect, assuming after King (2005, 2) that any exceedance of norms at either the artistic or ideological level must be associated with a certain distance and freedom from the restrictions imposed by the dominant production system. We must remember the utopian dimension that underlies the rhetoric of independence.

As was mentioned earlier, we are dealing here with a permanent state of crisis and hybridity that characterize production considered independent. This intensifies with the introduction of crowdfunding, which includes a new entity, fanvestors, in the process (Galuszka and Bystrov 2014). This change makes it necessary to redefine the position of the creator and analyze it from the perspective of the degree and method of using the topos of the independent artist as the basis for the "discursive structure." In such a system, "independence" can act as a marketing method, serving to consolidate fanvestors around the brand image (this can be considered a kind of tribal marketing, Cova and Cova 2002); therefore, the "motivating factor" function built on utopia is used. This evokes new problems since from the creators' perspective crowdfunding can be seen as a tool of "absolute" independence without an understanding of the specifics of this inverted production mechanism or their dependence on the financing community (Chapter 4 in this book shows that this can be problematic also in the case of musicians). Hence, the very creative process is subject to transformation, because it includes the collecting of funds, which becomes a significant element of the process of creating a film work from the artist's perspective. Let us add again: in the case of crowdfunding, this process is additionally included in the community context understood as co-creation, in which the recipients become co-creators of the film. The approach to independence as a discourse proposed by Tzioumakis is developed here through the context of social media and the broader issues of network communities. Built in the 1980s and 1990s, the image of an independent artist becomes the binding agent of the founding community, expanding the framework of the creative process. At the same time, it creates new challenges, especially when we consider other stages of the film's functioning – marketing and distribution. An example is the spectacular film campaign of *Veronica Mars* (Kickstarter 2013). The creators collected 5.7 million dollars, 3.7 million more than the assumed minimum sum. The project was supported by 91,585 people who, in exchange for their support, received various awards – from posters and DVDs to the possibility of naming one of the characters and receiving a role in the film ($10,000 contribution prize) (Goldstein and Morris 2013; Johnston 2013). Importantly, initially, the film was to be produced by Warner Bros., which withdrew, considering the project too risky. After the success of the Kickstarter campaign, the studio, which still owned the title, not only agreed to produce the film but offered support in its promotion and distribution. The main cause for the reversal of the studio's decision was the reaction of the fans, which promised a financial return. It is the question of this return that may be controversial. One could question the actual role of fanvestors also from a legal point of view.

As we have already said, the key factor when it comes to the specifics of crowdfunded cinema is the reversal of the production process (Berra 2008, 16) and the possibility of gradual commercialization in a form resembling "platform release" (King 2005, 26). In crowdfunding campaigns, this is related to exclusive access to specific content and with a slow gradation of campaign development activities. The word-of-mouth strategies are key here. It should be noted that the precursor in terms of its use in film production was *Blair Witch Project*. The creators of the film used the phenomenon described by Berra (2008, 87) in an extremely clever way, namely through the concealment of marketing by independent artists and the use of word-of-mouth. This type of promotion is treated by users as something "better" than traditional advertising and understood as a means of building a community of "the informed." It creates new possibilities for crowdfunding as a form of marketing, since:

> The niche audience is not opposed to marketing, but does not respond positively to the kind of blanket promotion that is characteristic of the studios.
>
> (Berra 2008, 163)

In the case of independent cinema, this community consists of cinephile viewers (Berra 2008, 181) and, more broadly, a niche audience, which may include "cult viewers," for example those associated with a particular genre (e.g. horror). An example of the latter is provided by the crowdfunding campaigns of the Troma company, which will be discussed later in the book.

The fanvestor understood in this way as a model recipient of independent cinema financed by crowdfunding fits into the characteristics that Berra (2008, 163–164) attributes to a niche market. In our opinion, key here are characteristics such as the "lack of competition or lack of attention and customer care from other companies" and "self-definition, to self-consciously avoid categorization amongst the 'mass.'" This means the existence of a "loyal" audience which does not threaten abandonment if it finds a "better" creator or film and (for some reason) defines itself as a niche audience – whether as a cinephile or cult/fan. In this way, it becomes an ideal target for tribal marketing (Cova and Cova 2002), which assumes a more subtle form in crowdfunding and refers to a community that is defined by the mere fact of participating in the campaign. This is part of the discourse of independence as the basis for film marketing of a specific type. It is worth noting that this bottom-up definition resulting from being "outside the corporate system" means that independence as a marketing tool is much more explicit than the category of actual filmmaking (Berra 2008, 201). Returning to describing the niche market, the following characteristic remains central, although they are subject to transformation: "sufficient size to be profitable and sustainable," "the potential for manageable growth," "the right level of income," and "opportunities for new companies to succeed based on instinctive knowledge of the market rather than pure financial acumen" (Berra 2008, 164). Because of the specifics of the campaign structure and methods of operating individual platforms, one should consider what "sufficient size" and "income" are for a given campaign. Since the audience takes part in the process of creation even at the level of production, its number of access points to the script increases. At the same time, many fanvestors pay very small amounts. This leads to a situation in which we are no longer talking about the film as a product but rather as a broadly understood service according to the paradigm of *service dominant logic* (Vargo and Lusch 2004, 2008).

The "instinctive knowledge" based on the recognition of the digital environment of a working community of recipients also gains special significance. Its correct recognition, in accordance with the specifics of communication on the web, leads to great possibilities for the development of this form of financing independent culture. Important here are issues related to the choice of platform, such as the possibility of payment of the collected sum (unless it has achieved the minimum assumed limit), the percentage charged by the platform, and the possibility of obtaining substantive assistance in the technical processing of the campaign on the platform. For example, the most popular platform, Kickstarter, does not offer the first or the third option, which increases risk by transferring to the creator the entire responsibility for the campaign – including the technical side (such as uploading of content). By contrast, Indiegogo allows for the use of raised funds even if the minimum amount has not been reached, making more risky projects possible (see Chapter 2 in this book).

However, this is not where the issue of transference of competencies to the creator ends. A crowdfunding campaign requires support at the word-of-mouth level. Projects can only succeed with the strong inclusion of social media – the number of campaigns is so large that it is not difficult to overlook them without an adequate response. A specific campaign must therefore be properly defined and boosted using keywords that will allow it to be included more often in search results, but it must also be encapsulated in an area of active, two-way communication with potentially interested recipients. All this is expected to boost traffic to the campaign website. The successful performance of this type of project, therefore, requires not only a large effort but also the expenditure of time and above all else competence in the use of social media – the employment of someone responsible for this sphere of the campaign. It is in this sphere, where the keywords and the communication channel with the recipient are defined, that the use of independence rhetoric is crucial, as it permits a campaign to reach the right niche market for the implementation of the project. Here, however, "instinctive knowledge" is absolutely linked to the technological context that affects the overall discourse. An interesting example is the so-called *gogofactor* – an algorithm that records all user activity on Indiegogo. The platform offers creators an environment of freedom, where projects are not selected by the administrators. However, this means that all responsibility for the activities around the project is transferred onto the creators themselves. As a consequence, this is the algorithm that determines the extent to which a given campaign will be promoted by the platform. Achieving a high result enables the placement of a campaign on the main page and in information sent by Indiegogo to social networking sites. The activity of other authors is also an important factor. Therefore, in addition to taking care of the activity related to their own project and fixing it in social media, creators should also follow the actions of others (Popiel 2011). This points to an additional context brought by crowdfunding to independent work. Of course, artists have always looked at the work of others, although in the rhetoric of independence bearing the signs of utopia, there appears in this element an assumed "lack of competition." In the model of crowdfunding, the inclusion of an additional factor, the operation of the algorithms of individual platforms, should also be considered. In this way, they are included in the network (as understood by Bruno Latour) of dependencies that make up the creative process of independent production.

The above issues indicate the types of changes to which independent film production is subject. In the following sections, we will briefly present three examples that we consider significant for the phenomenon of crowdfunding and which in our opinion illustrate its key aspects.

Zach Braff

The success of *Veronica Mars* aroused controversy regarding the role of large companies in the new financing model. However, it also became an inspiration for other creators with a recognized position in the world of independent film (Fishbein 2013). These include Zach Braff, who declared his desire to make the second part of his film *Garden State*, once recognized as both a generational manifesto and a cult film. The film had a budget of $2.5 million and was produced by Camelot Pictures, Jersey Films, Double Feature Films, and Large's Ark Productions. Distribution was handled by Fox Searchlight Pictures. Despite the fact that this arrangement guaranteed the maintenance of independence as part of the discourse (these companies were responsible for, among others, the films of Quentin Tarantino and Steven Soderbergh), it also maintained a close relationship with industry giants (News Corporation media group, to which Fox Searchlight Pictures belongs). This likely caused the creator not to be satisfied with the degree of independence he received with his first film, and the second film was to be created in a way that would guarantee "true independence." In this case, the use of crowdfunding became a manifesto of the filmmaker's artistic attitude. Inspired by the success of Rob Thomas and the film *Veronica Mars*, Braff presented a new form of financing as an opportunity for the implementation of "personal" and low-budget projects that would otherwise be threatened by a traditional financing system arranged by large studios. The campaign for the film *Wish I Was Here* raised $3.1 million from 46,520 people on the Kickstarter platform, while Braff himself declared that he financed most of the film (about $5 million) from his own funds (Goldstein and Morris 2013). In response to his appeal, he met not only with the positive reaction of fans but also numerous hateful reactions in social media (Zara 2013) because he was recognized as a "famous" artist and therefore had access to other forms of financing. In this case, the rhetoric of independence as part of crowdfunding could be understood through the prism of the lack of other sources of financing. This is illustrated by this fragment of an online review:

> Braff had been unable to find anyone willing to give him money so he turned to his fan base. In 48 hours, the film was fully funded, which speaks volumes about the love his fans have for what he does. But, again, that campaign launched a library of worried and sometimes angry think-pieces about crowdfunding (should it be used by famous people, especially someone like Braff who is so well-paid for his television work?), the state of movie-making, and all things Braff.
>
> (O'Malley 2014)

On the other hand, the popularity and the final funding of the project by the fan community point to discrepancies in this matter among recipients themselves as well as crowdfunding ambivalence. We are talking here about a "community" and a "bottom-up" form, although one ultimately associated with achieving certain profits. Interestingly, the reviewer here sees similarities with the creative strategy of Cassavetes, who, in her opinion, could now make his independent films using this form of financing. A reference to the film icon also gives a clear signal that it was this type of rhetoric that would shape the discussion of Braff's film.

The film was produced by Worldview Entertainment and Double Feature Films with a budget of $6 million and a box office of $5.5 million. Its distribution was handled by Focus Films – thus, again by a branch of a large group, this time NBC Universal. Therefore, for the context of the organization of production, its location does not mean complete detachment from large media concerns. Furthermore, the budget for distribution and promotion put forward by Focus Films far exceeded $6 million. Therefore, we are not talking about a "small, independent film," but quite a large undertaking, for which crowdfunding is a kind of flywheel and the first promotional platform attracting recipients in a niche market. The crowd constitutes a starting point for further promotional activities; therefore, attracting its attention is key for the success of the entire crowdfunding project. It is, then, a tool for measuring the interest of the audience. However, does it guarantee compliance with the expectations of viewers?

Let us look at the beginning of the trailer for the campaign. As we reported (Galuszka and Brzozowska 2016, 2017), this introduction to the campaign and later the degree of contact with recipients were key factors affecting its success. The trailer for Braff's film was made following a humorous convention that was legible to a specific audience – they were viewers who were fans of the previous film and were amused by their quirky humor *à la* the TV series *Scrubs*. There appear well-known faces, such as that of Jim Parsons of *Big Bang Theory,* so he was recognized by viewers completely unfamiliar with *Garden State*, and Donald Faison (whom viewers associated with *Scrubs*). Braff himself addresses the audience directly, presenting the film as a kind of continuation of *Garden State*, only better since it was realized with greater artistic freedom. The author speaks directly about the need to make concessions in the production of the previous film. Therefore, crowdfunding was to guarantee a truly independent character for the production. At this phase, an interesting paradox already appears. To illustrate how big studios work, Braff creates comedy scenes in which he frightens Parsons and Faison with the threat that people at the film studio would replace them with "real stars" – Justin Bieber and Denzel Washington. Braff refers here to the main strategies of large studios that build success using well-known names (Berra 2008, 58). Viewers are thereby defined as those who place themselves somewhat outside the mainstream and prefer to watch a film with "smaller caliber" actors better suited to their niche taste. However, Parsons and Faison were TV stars, and it is difficult to classify them as actors related to "niche" cinema. Interestingly, the female lead is played by Kate Hudson, while Parsons and Faison appear only in cameos. Therefore, we are dealing here with the use of independence rhetoric as a marketing ploy. Braff's campaign refers to a convention that his audience accepts, perhaps not reflecting on what that independence really is. The point is, as Levy rightly points out, there is "no longer an arthouse versus a mainstream audience" when "people going to see *Twister* are also seeing *Dead Man Walking*" (Levy 1999, 513). Braff seems to instinctively sense this trend and directs his message to the viewer who identifies with the generational message. In the trailer, the director speaks explicitly of the continuation of a generational statement, not so much in the sphere of a particular plot and hero but rather the experience of a certain age. It is not the same hero and story, but it could be since it combines generational experience. We may therefore speak about a defined receiving group of Braff's peers who expect an out-of-the-box presentation of their problems from the perspective of a "generational" director – let us add that we are talking about the audience who got used to a certain type of cinema in the 1990s, so in a sense, it is the "generation of Sundance" that flourished on a certain type of production it considered independent. The hero expected by this audience is characteristic of independent cinema discourse, which presents "insight into the lives of people who exist on the social fringes, and in doing so suggests why such characters make choices that would be considered to be anti-social by most audience members" (Berra 85).

But does the film *Wish I Was Here* fulfill the promises of the campaign trailer? Braff's film certainly refers to fan culture, as seen in the first scenes. There appear references to *Star Wars, Star Trek,* and *Game of Thrones,* and the development of the hero's attitude during the film is described from the perspective of the Jedi knight's narrative. The film also features a sequence, promised in the trailer, that takes place at Comic Con. This is an obvious bow toward the fan audience and fanvestors. However, it is difficult to escape the impression that these threads are rather marginal, and that in fact here we have a story about a farewell to fandom – even if references to it are constituted with an element of marital intimacy. The main character is mature – he is a decade older – and although he is not the same hero as in *Garden State*, we see some developmental consistency. We can also assume, after all, and according to Braff's intentions, that it shows the fate of a model representative of Generation X. This generation was shaped by fan culture, and it is still an important reference point for it; however, completely different problems dominate here, and these affect the overall mood of the film. One could say that *Wish I Was Here* tells a fairly classic, by Hollywood standards, a story of family reconciliation, acceptance of death, and adulthood. What is to distinguish it is the way of telling the story – from the perspective of a representative of the generation – and the introduction of elements that can be considered "disturbing" or mismatched (e.g. fandom threads and specific, sometimes dark humor). In this respect, the film is no different from its predecessor, although there is a clear intensification of the mood of pessimism with bitter conclusions. In contrast to the humorous tone of the trailer, the film ultimately presents something completely different, showing the unpleasant truth about growing up and having to accept the loss this brings. The similarities between the two films are therefore created at a subtle level and cannot be reduced to a formula of "even more Jim Parsons jokes." Continuity can also be seen in the musical layer and style. It should be emphasized that the "independent" overtones come down to a take on the story but not its form. We are therefore dealing with a classic tale of quite ordinary problems with an unusual hero. It is his specificity and the fact that the narrative is conducted from his perspective that contributes to the non-typical nature of this film, directed to an unusual, niche audience.

Finally, it is worth mentioning that the film received relatively low ratings from critics and a wider audience – 6.7 out of 10 on IMDB; on Rotten Tomatoes, the film holds a rating of 44%, based on 117 reviews; and on Metascore a score of 43 out of 100, based on 34 critics. Interestingly, critical opinions also emphasize generational issues, as exemplified by the following statement:

> Braff's Aidan represents a generation that was raised to do what makes them happy, but is now being told that that's not good enough.
> (IMDB 2014)

Even if the review is critical of model audiences, it certainly considers them a well-defined group. However, what ultimately becomes a problem is the suspension of the film between mainstream and independent cinema. Another critic points out that:

> Braff's sophomore effort arrives with a thud, another cog in the new American independent film machine, where its degree of visibility makes it not quite indie (perhaps it's best to leave any of your kickstarter funded criticisms at the door) and not quite mainstream.
> (Bell 2014)

This review indicates the ambiguous position of crowdfunding. On the one hand, thanks to the reversed order of undertaken actions and the specificity of directing a message to an existing community of viewers, it provides an opportunity to reach the niche audience. On the other hand, it shows that crowdfunding may be seen as responding to a "wide audience," suggesting that crowdfunded cinema has in fact an unclear status in the mainstream/independent system.

What is worse, this lack of recognition of the role of the audience is also visible, in this case, with the creator himself. The comments of fanvestors on the Kickstarter website clearly show the growing dissatisfaction with the effects of the campaign – but this is not about the film itself, since ratings were usually enthusiastic but rather about the lack of implementation of the promised awards and problems with privileged access to the film. As we mentioned in Chapter 2, due to the lack of any share in profits, awards that have an emotional dimension from a fan perspective are key in crowdfunding campaigns. This was the case here. Fans could therefore get, depending on the amount invested, rewards such as paraphernalia (e.g. t-shirts), collector's items (e.g. special vinyl records of the soundtrack), or the opportunity to meet the creators at the premiere. A particularly important award were screenings, which allowed contributors to watch the film prior to the official distribution. It was obvious that the rewards were tailored to a fan audience that defined itself as niche and cult. The creators, however, showed a total misunderstanding of their role in this system and failed to fulfill campaign promises. A major part of post-campaign comments expressed complaints and dissatisfaction resulting from not receiving the promised rewards – with comments published as recently as seven months of this writing, which indicates that nothing was done to address this. Comments show that fans were completely aware of both their role and its limitations. Emotional capital (Jenkins 2006) is in the foreground and is referred to directly. An expression of extreme desperation is the following statement from the forum on the campaign website:

> Hey there, I have still received nothing ... please ... PLEASE do something for us who believed in you and gave you our hard-earned money ... at least, out of respect for us!
> (Kickstarter 2015d)

An analysis of comments in chronological order shows a gradual decrease in both excitement and willingness to take part in a joint creative process (e.g. comments on changes in the cast, the latest photos from the set, trailers, or even suggesting specific positions for the soundtrack. In their place is bitterness resulting from a lack of contact (posts representing Braff and Coco become less frequent, especially when problems with sending prizes and screenings start) and the fulfillment of promises. Moreover, users point to copyright issues as exemplified by the following statement from the forum on the campaign website:

> The movie is online pirated in many different languages, so everyone in the world has been able to see this. Before the people that helped pay for it.
> (Kickstarter 2014a)

Users even talk about the possibility of going to court as pointed out in this statement:

> [...] so it's better to not get sued by the copyright holders than being sued by individuals Kickstarter backers outside the US? Do you see the irony of how Zach Braff is destroying Kickstarter for independent filmmakers?
> (Kickstarter 2014b)

Fanvestors as a niche audience, therefore, demonstrate a high awareness of their role in the new arrangement of crowdfunded cinema. We are not talking here about a naive audience that "can be bought" thanks to marketing tricks using the rhetoric of independence. On the contrary, we have viewers who are thoroughly aware of the difficulties encountered by creators of this type of cinema but who at the same time demand recognition of their role in the process of co-creation. This case clearly shows that a total success and new model of crowdfunding cinema can be discussed only when the creator fully understands the role of the audience and is aware of the fact that it is an active part of the entire process and not merely a sponsor.

Troma

An entirely different situation exists in the case of Troma Entertainment, a film production and distribution company founded in the 1970s known for its low-budget B horror movies. Its best-known titles, including *TheToxic Avenger* and *Surf Nazis Must Die*, have attracted a faithful following of fans who thirst for the macabre, sex, and ostentatiously unrealistic special effects. Troma was set on a cult reception and the active participation of viewers in the filmmaking process from the very beginning. Thus, crowdfunding is nothing new for Troma. It was a natural development of its already existing relations with fans. From its inception, Troma existed mainly thanks to private investors and creators' own outlay. This, in conjunction with the involvement of a faithful audience, allowed it to survive in a market dominated by big budget productions. Contact with fans was important to the studio from day one, and it is for this reason that its founders paid close attention to managing a website and quickly became interested in the potential of social networks to strengthen those contacts. In this case, crowdfunding was a logical development of activities it was already carrying out.

In recent years, the situation of the company has significantly worsened, a situation caused by, among other things, changes in independent film distribution. In response, members and enthusiasts of Troma began to look for new methods of financing and expanded media contact with fans. The first crowdfunding experiment was the campaign *TROMA Entertainment Return to Nuke 'Em High DUCK-STARTER!* It was signed by Tromadance Film Festival. The campaign, which aimed to finance a performance in the movie by a professionally trained duck named Kevin, was successful: $10,192 pledged by 95 backers of a $4,000 goal. The entertaining promotion of the campaign refers to the strategy of employing stars as pointed out in this fragment of the campaign description:

> Just like any A-list celebrity, KEVIN has his back-stage demands. Troma usually makes low-budget movies, and trained animal actors usually only appear in huge films like Jurassic Park, Lord of the Rings and Star Wars! KEVIN is a star, and only fans of "reel" art can make it possible for KEVIN to appear in Troma's movie.
> (Kickstarter 2012b)

From the start, the campaign was built on a strong rhetoric of independence and reference to a well-defined niche audience. Creativity was opposed to Hollywood productions based on the star system. At the same time, the film was immediately situated into an area of cult perception as a "revisiting of the 1980s cult classic," and the president of the company, Lloyd Kaufman, is presented in promotional materials as a legendary figure. Therefore, this message has a very specific addressee, one who has probably been involved in Troma's activities before.

Encouraged by its first crowdfunding success, Kaufman decided to make a documentary, *Occupy Cannes!*, which was to present attempts to rent a cinema during the famous festival in order to present *Return to Nuke'Em High* (whose star was Kevin). The campaign was to cover the costs of travel and presentation as well as documenting the entire undertaking. The goal was therefore to demystify the film distribution process. To quote Kaufman: "We will make a documentary film that will show how this festival – and the idea of the film festival in general – have been distorted" (Rothman 2013). Although the project did not reach the minimum assumed amount ($50,000 – ultimately, $30,683 was achieved from 385 backers), thanks to the contributions of the creators themselves it was successful. Importantly, the Indiegogo platform was used, making it possible to use part of the funds raised. The film was realized, and one Cannes festival commentator described it as "a pean for part of the independent cinema and a shout of protest against the corporate consolidation of the film industry" (Davidzon 2013). Despite its apparent failure, this project can be considered a success. First, the choice of the platform allowed for the use of collected funds, even when the entire declared sum was not collected, and the risk of project failure was minimized (it is likely that the developers were aware that this project was riskier than others and, knowing that the production differed from typical Troma films, they did not want to expose the audience to this risk). In this way, crowdfunding simply supported the current model of Troma's operation. Second, contact with the fanbase was also strengthened, which probably allowed for the implementation of a fully successful campaign on Kickstarter, *Return to Nuke 'Em High: Volume 2*. In this case, with the support of 959 backers, $63,615 was collected from the predeclared $50,000. It is worth mentioning that this third campaign did not assume covering the total cost of film production but only postproduction and possibly distribution (if the minimum amount were exceeded – which it was). The developers specified these goals on the project website as illustrated by this fragment of the campaign description:

> We've keep costs down (our entire budget less than 1% of your typical Hollywood movie) but we are now faced with the final hurdle. All that remains are the post production costs: sound mixing, color correction, editing, special effects, mastering, etc.
>
> [...]
>
> If the event that your support exceeds our post-production expenses, every dollar donated over our $50,000 mark will go towards distributing this film in theaters as widely as possible.
>
> (Kickstarter 2015e)

With such an honest approach combined with a truly loyal cult audience, the discussion of organizational shortcomings was different from that surrounding Braff's campaign. Of course, one can find a number of comments expressing dissatisfaction with the lack of rewards received and the film being produced by the expected date. However, these are much more subdued, and visible is the phenomenon of internal censorship in the group – an example is the discussion between users Jessie stein and Julphagor (original spelling) (Kickstarter 2015f).

Close contact with the fans and building emotional capital as a weapon in a market dominated by high-budget productions were crucial for the company's existence from the very beginning. This is clearly visible in how the company's website is designed (www.troma.com) with its links to profiles on social media (Facebook, Twitter, Tumblr). The transition to individual social pages shows Troma's incredible activity and at the same time its strong connection with the activities of fans – the specificity of the company's activities is based on the fact that it is difficult to clearly indicate the border between fan activity and the "main text." Troma and especially Kaufman also undertake numerous activities to promote fans' own film work. This is visible in, for example, YouTube lessons and the Horror Film Challenge organization, but also by the announcement published on the website that Troma undertakes to distribute films produced by fans. The recognition by the company of the possibilities offered by social media finds its representation in the change of the main slogan from "Almost 40 years of reel independence" to "45 years of disrupting media." Creative independence is therefore realized here through a series of complex actions in social media and as part of live meetings (convents, parties, etc.) that are a natural consequence of the cult perception model. However, the consistent reference to the discourse of independence, which is based on an ironic game with the recipient, is extremely original here. The juxtaposition of exaggerated slogans about creative freedom and the nature of Troma's work can give a comic effect, which is well played by the head of the company who appears as a cult figure in promotional materials and at meetings with fans. Paradoxically, thanks to its film production model, which has been on the verge of bankruptcy for years, in terms of its production system Troma actually achieves creative independence at all levels. Furthermore, taking into account the declared and strong fanbase, crowdfunding is a natural consequence and phase of development.

Interesting in this context is the factual and honest approach of Lloyd Kaufman to the new form of financing. Troma has engaged in several campaigns, the most original of which was *Occupy Cannes!,* a promotional campaign. Placing it on Indiegogo shows that the creators were aware that it did not stand a chance of fully succeeding – and surely, this was not the goal. In his statements as the head of the company, Kaufman stresses that crowdfunding cannot be a way to fully fund movies (even when talking about those with low budgets) (Rothman 2013). Crowdfunding can therefore rather act as a marketing tool in support of traditional forms of film promotion. At the same time, it may also serve to research potential markets through probing audience likes and preferences. In this way, crowdfunding becomes an extension of the rhetoric of independence as the basis for building film marketing.

In the case of Troma, what is probably most significant is that crowdfunding has become an additional channel for binding a cult audience with the company and allowing this audience greater participation in the creative process. The approach here is based on Kaufman's understanding that independence (as part of the film production and distribution system) does not mean independence from viewers' opinions and their willingness to actively contribute to the creation of the film. While 45 years of building Troma's emotional capital is strongly inscribed here in the context of cult cinema and fan culture, it is the discourse of independence that unites the community of recipients that distinguishes this work from the enormity of class B productions.

Sekielski brothers

The final example that we would like to draw upon here is the production by brothers Tomasz and Marek Sekielski *Tylko nie mów nikomu* (2019) (*Tell No One*) This example is slightly different, since it does not apply to independent cinema in a strict sense but rather to a journalistic documentary. We reference it because it is the most famous Polish documentary in recent years, and it was realized in conditions of total systemic independence from film studios and TV stations (which in the Polish system often cooperate in film productions). We also find interesting the use of a slightly different crowdfunding model offered by the Patronite platform. This introduces additional threads in the discussion on the role of fanvestors that are important from the perspective of independence in general.

The theme of the documentary is the sexual abuse of minors by priests and the concealment of this by the Polish Catholic Church. The construction of the film is based on direct accounts of the victims and their attempts to confront them with the perpetrators. However, there are no Church hierarchs in the film, because none agreed to participate. It can already be seen that the film was extremely controversial, and although this issue does not concern Poland exclusively (it exists in Ireland, the United States, and elsewhere), in Poland it comes to a specific ground in connection with the strong connection between the Polish Catholic Church and state authorities. Hence, it was clear from the beginning that the Sekielski brothers would not be able to realize their documentary in the mainstream. Not only did they not count on the cooperation of public media (controlled by the authorities), they were aware that private TV stations were afraid of a scandal. Problems would return in relation to distribution, which we will discuss.

The creators decided on a specific form of crowdfunding offered by the portal Patronite, a Polish equivalent of Patreon (2018). Its model of operation is slightly different from Kickstarter platforms, as it focuses on constantly supporting a specific artist and his or her work. However, as with the case of other platforms, fans receive unique rewards from creators. Since the matter concerns primarily artistic projects, most often these involve unpublished or limited materials (e.g. by comic book artists or cartoonists). Youtubers and podcast creators also constitute a large segment, which makes the platform an ideal vehicle for the development of citizen journalism. A particularly important feature, which applies to the example discussed here, is its focus on the creator. The Patronite model is more "fan-focused" than the Kickstarter model and is based directly on the relationship with a given creator. As in the previous examples, there, too, the issues of emotional capital and relations with the creator play a substantial role, but here this element is strengthened thanks to the stability brought by the subscription mechanism and fixed fees (rather than a one-off payment for a specific action). In this way, the fan community does in fact become a community of patrons who in a real way "provide for" the creator. From the perspective of the funded creator, this carries even greater risk in the event of this community's dissatisfaction, which believes that it has the right to decide on the nature of creativity and to hold the creator accountable for what he or she does. The relationship between creators and the communities that finance them is delicate, which is especially important when we talk about online celebrities.

In the case of Tomasz Sekielski, the case appeared somewhat different, since for years he had been a well-known journalist with a large group of loyal readers and viewers. The transfer of funding to the crowdfunding platform, which was supposed to mean actual independence from television stations, of course, entailed a certain risk, though it was perhaps a natural consequence of an existing relationship with the recipients. The relationship was enhanced and formalized by the project, and following the realization of the film, Sekielski's profile continues to enjoy great popularity, and he plans to realize more documentaries. As of November 2019, the author had 2,463 patrons and received monthly payments of PLN88,760 (approximately $22,800), with altogether PLN1,398,870 collected so far (around $360,540). The film *Tell No One* was realized for the sum of PLN450,000 (approx. $115,000) collected from 2,500 people. Patrons can receive various rewards depending on the degree of financial commitment: from satisfaction resulting from "approaching the truth" to access to an exclusive Facebook group and other typical crowdfunding rewards such as limited materials, invitations to shows, and autographs. The formulation of the messages regarding subsequent prize levels is noteworthy. Thresholds are marked with slogans indicating the "active" dimension of the recipients' activity. Horizontal headings are: "Ask," "Discover," "Inquire," "Verify," "Analyze," "Confront," "Condemn," and "Speak Loudly" (Patronite 2018).

The concept of independence is therefore also introduced here from the side of the recipient, who is characterized by a desire for independent thought and action. Such a formulation prompts the audience to feel part of the process, and linking these slogans with specific rewards is rather symbolic. When defining their audience, the brothers probably assumed that it would consider the rewards as secondary to the joint mission of "reaching the truth." This activity understood as a joint process of co-creation must take place in the conditions of a release from a dependence on the media and political system. In the case of the campaign for *Tell No One* on Patronite, we can speak of a kind of DIY community and "communal evaluation," which, along with the development of social news, can contribute to a change in the balance of power in the field of journalism (Poell and van Dijck 2015).

Since we are talking about a documentary that is at the same time a journalistic investigation, we must take this aspect into account. It is worth paying attention, after Bennett (2015, 10), to the relationality of the concept of independence, when we consider issues such as links with the left or right side of a political scene. One may wonder whether in this case the context of "alternative media" as a counter-hegemonic formula in relation to mainstream media should be discussed. This is supported by an emphasis on both bottom-up action and commitment as well as political overtones. As Bennett writes:

> alternative media tend to be leftist, if not socialist in orientation and predominantly take the form of initiatives in journalism or informing and mobilizing a political public: they are inherently participatory, grassroots, counter-hegemonic, nonhierarchical, one-to-one, small scale and on the margins. Particularly through digital tools and technologies, alternative media – in their utopian visions – promise to provide marginalized and disenfranchised groups with a platform and a voice [...] alternative media promise participation through the media, independent media are still more likely to conform to promoting participation in the media (12)

In turn, Christian Fuchs notes that "alternative media studies are strongly connected to Anarchist perspectives" (2010, 174). Considering this, it is difficult to consider the Sekielskis' film alternative media, because there is certainly no anarchist perspective. We are not speaking of a marginalized group in the sense of subculture but rather of specific individuals who, as victims, have not been given justice.

Surely, the purpose of the campaign was "mobilizing a political public," where the concept of independence is firmly embedded in a broader political discourse. However, this public does not necessarily have to be leftist, because voices of opposition to the attitude of Church hierarchs can also be found on the right side of the political scene, to which we will return in a moment. It follows that the conservative audience is not excluded as a target.

In the context of the alternative media, it is worth mentioning that the concept of participation is not free from controversy, as pointed out by researchers such as Christian Fuchs and José van Dijck. Since we are speaking of a voluntary activity pursued in free time, it is susceptible to exploitation in a new form: free labor (Terranova 2000). In the case of crowdfunding, of course, the situation is somewhat different, because even though we are talking about a sort of DIY community, its operation is actually limited to funding and support built on the relationship with the creator (Galuszka and Brzozowska 2016, 2017; see also Chapter 2 in this book). In the case of the Sekielskis' film, it seems that both factors are equally important, which highlights certain features present on other crowdfunding platforms and in the examples in the previous sections. The authors faced not only potential financial disaster but also social ostracism and possible legal consequences resulting from people who cared about the phenomenon presented in the film.

It is particularly important in this context that the video is available for free on YouTube (YouTube 2019); therefore, from the very beginning, it was not geared towards financial return. The video was placed on Sekielskis' YouTube channel, which is part of the Videobrothers.tv partner network, on 11 May 2019. In less than 6 hours, it broke the Polish YouTube viewership record with over a million views. A day later the number of views was already over 10 million, and in one week it had 20 (Pallus 2019; Grzegorczyk 2019). The film had a total of 450,000 positive ratings and 23,000 negative in the YouTube system (i.e. thumbs up and down). Importantly, the film is shown not only for free but also without ads.

Since the beginning, the matter of its distribution aroused controversy. At first, no large TV station wanted to broadcast it – despite the fact that the Sekielski brothers offered the film with a free license for emission. Four days after its success on YouTube, TV WP showed it, and it reached an audience of 170,000 viewers in this first broadcast – setting a record for this station for viewership of one program (Kurdupski 2019). A day later, the film was broadcast by the largest private station, TVN. On average, the documentary was watched on TVN by over 2.2 million viewers – of all viewers, one in three turned on the TV during its broadcast. The average audience was therefore 2.24 million people, and the film was the 11th most popular television program of the week, ahead of, among others, the most popular news programs – TVP1's *Wiadomości* (*The News*; 2.16 million viewers), Polsat's *Wydarzenia* (*Current Events*; 2.13 million) – and entertainment – the TV show *Koło fortuny* (*Wheel of Fortune*) and the series *Na sygnale* (*Sirens*; 2.13 million each). TVN's competitor Polsat had only 380,000 viewers at the time of its broadcast. Importantly, TVN also broadcast the movie without interrupting it with commercials. (Pallus 2019). Therefore, one can observe how the discourse of independence, in this case, influenced the strategies of commercial stations, which initially showed little interest. After the success of its free broadcast on YouTube, they tried to take part in it, using a wave of interest, but not in an ostentatious way (i.e. no ads).

With such viewership, it is also worth mentioning the reception, which was varied both on the side of the Church hierarchs and representatives of the government and among the audience. Upon the realization of the scale of the film's popularity, official reactions took on a diplomatic note, although one of the most significant in the initial period following the broadcast was the statement of one of the most important Polish Church hierarchs: asked by journalists whether he had seen the film, he said that "he does not watch baloney." Despite the fact that later this statement was suppressed, it became for many a symbol of the contemptuous position of the Church towards the victims of pedophile priests. Finally, the Permanent Council of the Polish Episcopal Conference issued an official announcement that stated the following: "The film, taking the perspective of the victims, made us all aware of the magnitude of their suffering" (Konferencja Episkopatu Polski, 26 May 2019). Minor actions were taken against perpetrators, such as the abolition of pastoral status or removal of a figure from a monument. A special team of prosecutors was also appointed to investigate the events depicted in the film.

Differentiation can also be seen when we view the comments under the YouTube video (YouTube 2019). Critical comments on Sekielskis' work are a minority and they indicate for example that the phenomenon is not characteristic of the Church. Interesting diversity is visible from the perspective of represented views. We read, therefore, both statements that in a direct (and often vulgar) way declare atheistic and anti-clerical views and others by people who describe themselves as believers and as such are appalled by the phenomenon. Furthermore, differences can be seen in the language used by the commentators. We find both a style typical of internet discussions, full of vulgarity, devoid of Polish diacritical signs, and characterized by a direct form of addressing the interlocutor, as well as a style built in full sentences with correct spelling and polite forms. This indicates the differentiation of viewers also in terms of age and way of using the internet. The last level of differentiation is the diversity of national language; after the addition of foreign-language subtitles, the film also became popular abroad (especially in Ireland).

Of course, the audience commenting on YouTube is broader than that which makes up the community of Patrons. For this community, Sekielski has a clear message that he continues with reference to the next films he is producing. In his words, Patronite, through access to a closed group on Facebook, is to become a "platform for substantive discussion." Furthermore, in his thanks in the first campaign, Sekielski addresses "the community of creators" of the future films and he states that it takes great courage to act like this considering the political situation (Patronite 2019). A strategy is clearly visible, which is not only built on the rhetoric of independence in relation to a precisely defined recipient. In this case, it is not as much an "art house" or "cult" but rather the recipient representing certain intellectual values personified by the ideal of investigative journalism, but also inclined to the substantive discussion. In this way the niche nature of this discussion is created, which is emphasized by the possibility of participating in a closed exclusive group on Facebook. What is also striking is the indication of fanvestors literally as "filmmakers" (not even co-creators). In this way, Sekielski, who stresses at every turn that he is an independent producer and journalist, gives a clear signal that he understands that this independence is not absolute and that the new document creation model involves co-creation. Importantly, in this particular case, co-creation goes beyond financing, since it includes this discussion as an important element of communication between the creator and recipients, and includes the creative process itself. It is difficult to speak of free labor in this case; rather, we are talking about an inspiring discussion on both sides, the consequence of which is a film not targeted at profit.

The ideological diversity among the commentators mentioned above also does not allow for easy placement of the Sekielski brothers' actions within the cited definitions of alternative media. Certainly, however, *Tell No One* is linked to the independent cinema by a striving to introduce the viewer to a kind of discomfort resulting from the alternative presentation of certain themes, even if these themes are already recognizable in mainstream productions. The extraordinary popularity of this film has permitted the exposure to a broad audience of the impact of a strategy, which is directed as part of the discourse of independence to a niche audience. Complete financial independence in the case of this production combined with a conscious and thought-through inclusion of viewers into a substantive discussion on the problems presented enabled the creation of a precedent that may change the approach to documentary film and create real conditions for communal evaluation.

Notes

1 According to Levy, a contradiction of this and, therefore, a symbolic end of Generation X in cinema is the 1997 film *Good Will Hunting* (508).
2 And this is why Levy completely omits Class B films (Levy 1999).

4 Crowdfunding and independence in music

Theorizing independence in music

Understanding independence in music: Economic criteria

In the second half of the 20th century, independence was a concept defined in several ways. Its most common, but at the same time not very precise, understanding accentuated the dichotomy of independent label versus major record label. Therefore, to understand what independent music labels are and what they are not, we should have a closer look at the major record companies. Looking from the perspective of several decades, it should be noted that the very concept of a major record company did not mean the same specific companies but simply encompassed largest entities, whose names and owners were changing. Since the 1980s, major record companies should be viewed on a global scale, as a number of big corporations operating in all relevant markets and controlling approximately 70% of the global recording market.

In the second half of the 20th century, the key to maintaining major record companies' advantage over other market participants was their control of their own distribution networks. The establishment of such a network, especially in large countries, was a task that required significant capital expenditure, which meant that only the largest players could afford it. Smaller companies could either enter into distribution cooperation with the largest entities, use the services of independent distributors, or try alone or in cooperation with other small entities to build their own distribution network. Since the distribution of physical media was crucial for the functioning of a record company in the second half of the 20th century (it was difficult to sell albums if they were not available in stores), the distinction regarding who distributes the products of a given company became the basis for defining what an independent record label is. A truly independent label was therefore seen as one that did not have any distribution agreements with a major record company (Passman 2019).

This understanding of independence had, for some time, a significant advantage: a clear distinguishing criterion. The application of the distribution criterion – "independent" is what is distributed without cooperation with major labels – has enabled the creation of independent record charts based on reports from independent distributors. This is how the official British list of independent labels was created, which debuted in the industry magazine *Business Record* in January 1980 (Fonarow 2006, 33). The creation of such a list was of significant promotional importance because placing works on the list allowed artists whose work was released by independent labels to introduce themselves to a wider audience without having to compete with artists supported by the major record companies. However, the importance of distribution as a criterion for distinguishing independent releases decreased at the turn of the 1980s and 1990s when major record labels realized that "[a]ny major corporation could have an independent band by distributing the record through one of the independent distribution companies" (Fonarow 2006, 37). One of the practices used by major record companies was to establish crypto-independent labels, which were owned by large companies and benefited from their promotional and financial support, but whose releases were distributed by independent distributors. This made it possible to place on the list of independent releases products that were de facto releases of major record companies. As a result, even before the spread of the internet, using distribution as a criterion to distinguish independent labels from major record companies had become problematic (Negus 1999).

A similar way of defining independence is to take into account the existence of ownership relationships between a small label and major record companies. Following this thought, an independent label should be defined as a label that is independent from major record companies in terms of capital, i.e. a major has no shares in the label. This eliminates the crypto-independents from the independent music labels, but it does not exclude the existence of any cooperation between the small label and a major record company. At first glance, ownership seems to be a criterion consistent with an intuitive understanding of how capitalism works – it may be difficult for a small label acquired by a major record company to convince the audience that it still retains its independence. The problem, however, is that in the contemporary music market there are many opportunities for cooperation between these entities, and these go far beyond simple ownership relations. For example, a small label established in Italy may not have any capital or distribution relationships with major record companies elsewhere in Europe, but, at the same time, the rights to release a part of its catalog in other territories (e.g. in the USA, Asia) may be transferred on the basis of a long-term license contract with a major record company. Moreover, such a contract may only apply to physical media in some countries but, in other countries, also to intangible media. The level of complexity will be raised even higher when we take into account the existence of many other rights that a small music company may have (and therefore, it may grant licenses for them or sell them), e.g. the right to synchronize sound with an image. It clearly shows that the application of 20th century criteria for defining independence in music to contemporary realities can be problematic.[1]

To make the picture even more complex, let us imagine an artist who has not signed a record contract with any music label. Can this artist be automatically regarded as independent? The answer to this question is not possible if we do not know how the artist gets funds for his activity. If his career is financed by a sponsorship agreement with a large organization operating outside the music industry, then perhaps he does not have direct, indisputable power over his repertoire decisions. But, is this situation actually synonymous with total loss of artistic independence?

This does not mean that economic criteria, such as distribution and ownership, should not be used at all. It still makes sense today to look at what type of capital stands behind a given release, but it should be supplemented by other criteria. A good starting point in our search for these criteria could be the answer to the question of why we value independence in the first place, and where the widely spread view that "independent" means "artistically valuable" comes from.

Why is independence highly valued?

Despite the fact that when referring to an artist or a music label, the term "independent" often means "lacking funds to employ the best producers, session musicians, etc.," this concept, rather than being associated with permanent underinvestment, usually raises positive feelings. It is true that, from a financial point of view, independent record labels often operate in difficult conditions. Therefore, a justified question arises: where does the common conviction of the artistic superiority of their releases come from? Why would "independent," however defined, be better than "dependent," "commercial," or "mainstream" (although these terms are not synonymous)?

Crowdfunding and independence in music 65

An answer to these questions is possible if we look at meanings conferred to independence through the prism of Pierre Bourdieu's theory of the field of cultural production (1993). His research concerned most of all the book market. Nevertheless, during the last three decades, his theoretical concepts have been successfully applied to other types of cultural production, including music. According to Bourdieu, cultural producers can be driven either by market logic, according to which success is expressed in economic terms, or by "art for art's sake" logic, which emphasizes recognition from a closed circle of connoisseurs and peer artists. The latter was called by Bourdieu "the economic world reversed" (1983, 311) as it condemned attempts to make cultural products with the purpose of earning economic profit. This dichotomy has its roots in Romanticism, when the autonomy of creators (at that time mostly writers) from their pre-capitalist patrons was shaping (see also Hesmondhalgh 2013). Not seeking economic profit is therefore seen as giving artists autonomy from the dominant field of economic power. As Moore put it, in the case of independent music, "success is measured not in terms of the 'economic capital' of sales and profits but rather the 'symbolic capital' of making good art that is recognized by peers and critics" (2007, 468). The field of cultural production is a place of constant struggle over what art is "legitimate" and what is "commercial," and the boundaries of the field are constantly redefined. It is in this context that we should interpret discussions of whether a particular artist is "mainstream" or a label "sold-out."

Apart from non-commercialism, authenticity is often seen as an attribute of independent artists. In a highly simplified way, it can be assumed that one way of understanding authenticity in relation to an individual artist concerns "the supposed reasons she [the artist] has for working, whether her primary felt responsibility is to herself, her art, her public, or her bank balance" (Moore 2002, 211). Although most of us cannot completely avoid the "responsibility to bank balance," this quote clearly illustrates the essence of the commercial versus non-commercial dichotomy, which is one of the aspects of understanding independence in popular music.

Anti-commercialism is also one of the elements of authenticity mentioned by Marshall:

- "Anti-commercialism.
- An (at best) ambivalent relationship to technological development.
- Emphasis upon individual expression and originality.
- Emphasis upon the instinctiveness/non-rational nature of music.

- An allegiance to the black roots of the music.
- An emphasis on the personal nature of the relationship between performer and listener.
- An emphasis on live performance.
- An emphasis on the relationship between the performer and his/her community" (2005, 65–66).

Not all of the criteria listed by Marshall will be relevant to our analysis. To what extent recipients appreciate authenticity, and to what extent individual criteria are taken into account depends on the genre of music and the career development of a given artist. For example, the contradiction that occurs between the fact that the rock musician is to be noncommercial on the one hand and, on the other hand, his popularity brings him financial success, can be neutralized by other characteristics of the artist, e.g. the quality of his interaction with the audience during live performances. Authenticity understood as a quality composed of many elements is crucial for understanding the concept of independence.

Music released by independent music labels is perceived as more authentic, inter alia because small record labels are less often perceived from the perspective of money making than large companies. Of course, it is difficult to generalize, but it can be assumed that for some of the audience it is important that a large music label is managed by a hired manager, who sometimes comes from outside the music industry, while the small label is managed by an artist, music fan, or enthusiast. For a major record label, the criteria of revenue, market share, and profitability will be key when making repertoire decisions, whereas, for small labels, the diversity of attitudes regarding economic criteria and making money is greater. Because there are thousands of small labels, we can find among them both those for whom making money is not very important, and those that approach this issue in the same way as large major record labels. Hesmondhaldh noted that the extension of the positive perception of independence onto all independent labels took place already in the 1960s and 1970s:

> The discourses of fans, musicians and journalists during the countercultural heyday of rock and soul in the 1960s and 1970s saw "independents," small record companies with no ties to vertically integrated corporations, as preferable to the large corporations because they were less bureaucratic and supposedly more in touch with the rapid turnover of styles and sounds characteristic of popular music at its best. Such companies were

often, in fact, even more exploitative of their musicians than were the major corporations. (1999, 35)

This quote shows that the positive image of music independence that has been in existence since the 1960s was partly based on subjective interpretations of the artistic quality of the recordings. Observations made by musicians, critics, and fans about the higher quality of recordings issued by small music labels were imposed on the aforementioned commercial versus noncommercial dichotomy, which led to the conviction of the artistic superiority of independent labels. The fact that small labels often exploited musicians more than major record companies did, as noted by Hesmondhalgh (1999), was largely overlooked.

A significant change in the understanding of independence in music came with the birth of punk music in the second half of the 1970s, which was accompanied by the do-it-yourself ethos (DIY) and the subsequent development of post-punk independents in the 1980s. The factor favorable for the development of the independent scene at that time was the fact that the conviction that involvement and participation are crucial encountered favorable economic factors – falling costs of renting recording studios and pressing vinyl. As a result, independent release and distribution of records became activities that were feasible without access to large capital (Dunn 2012). The do-it-yourself attitude was largely the result of the politically motivated awareness that it was necessary to build an alternative to the mainstream music industry. This awareness was based, among other things, on the belief that "independent ownership of production *and* distribution was the most effective route towards democratization of the industry" (Hesmondhalgh 1999, 37) emphasis as in the original.

The artistic and economic success of independent labels in the USA and the UK in the 1980s contributed, however, to blurring of the understanding of independence in popular music. In a sense, it was part of the earlier trend of the 1960s and 1970s. At that time, smaller labels with valuable assets (e.g. exclusive rights to release recordings of an attractive artist, a promising record catalog) were taken over by larger companies. As noted by Negus:

The absorption of independent labels has been a feature of the music business throughout the twentieth century and has become increasingly institutionalized through a series of joint ventures, production, licensing, marketing and distribution deals, which have led to the blurring of "indie"/"major" organizational distinctions and belief systems. (1999, 35)

In the early 1990s, a number of labels from the punk and post-punk scene underwent the same fate – they went bankrupt or were taken over by major record companies. From that time comes the famous quote by the founder of Creation Records, Alan McGee, who said: "There's only two things that happen with independent labels ... you either get bought out or die. And that's it. There is no middle ground" (Hesmondhalgh 1999, 51). This quote touches on the core of the issue of authenticity because it indicates that there are only two things that may happen to an independent label following its success: selling out or bankruptcy. However, we should consider the possibility that, although this quote was well suited to the realities of the 1990s, today the word "independence" is comprehensive enough to cover, at least in the common sense, various forms of ad hoc cooperation with large entities, even from those outside the music industry. Dale writes about the diversity of today's independents and, comparing Domino Records – the label behind the successes of the band Franz Ferdinand, among others – with small entities such as Small Wonder and Dischord, he proposes that the latter be called DIY independents (2008, 185). Taking into account the variety of types of music independence, such a distinction – between dynamic independent labels driven mostly by economic logic and DIY independents that emphasize ideological aspects such as autonomy – seems necessary. This is particularly important in the context of the growing importance of social media, which adds to blurring the distinction between what is mainstream and what is niche (Suhr 2012).

The question of how independence should be defined today is important in relation to crowdfunding – on the one hand, this form of financing musical activity allows artists to function without the support of large entities but, on the other hand, crowdfunding is inherently associated with money, and this is money that becomes one of the main topics of communication between the creator and fans. Later, we will come back to the difficult relationship between independence and the strictly financial side of crowdfunding.

Why independence, and what kind is needed today?

As we mentioned earlier, the concept of independence is more complex and difficult to encompass today than in the second half of the 20th century. It does not change the fact that in the realities of today's music market, independence, understood as being motivated in one's cultural activities by something more than the simple need to make a profit, is very much needed. To properly understand the challenges that musicians face today and the answer that could be given by a modern-day understanding of independence, we will continue to ponder what qualities characterize independence. Based on earlier works of Hesmondhalgh (1997, 1999) and on more recent sources (Brown 2012; Dale 2008; Dunn 2012; Marshall 2005; Moore 2007; Strachan 2007), we propose a set of largely timeless characteristics, such as:

- The existence of an acquaintance or a personal relationship between a record company and an artist;
- The need to be more active, the need for mobilization and participation;
- Awareness of the need to build a community of recipients;
- The need to document artistic achievements;
- Fairer fund distribution rules;
- Informal contracts;
- Self-management – "production, distribution, and promotion on the artists' own terms" (Brown 2012, 524)
- "Noncorporate ethos" (Dunn 2012, 229); and
- The "business model is not one defined by profit-maximization" (Dunn 2012, 231)

Cammaerts points out similar components of independence:

> A more equal sharing of profit among the whole work force involved in the creative process, a shared ideological culture between artist and record label, the participation of artists in the running and functioning of the record label, the development of alternative and genuinely independent distribution channels and the adoption of a distinct aesthetic mirroring this different attitude and ideology to music production and distribution. (2010, 7)

Of course, this does not mean that independent artists and labels are not allowed to earn money or else they lose their independent status. Ignoring the economic aspects of business is a straight path to bankruptcy or to being forced to sell shares to a larger entity, and this is exactly what happened to independent labels in the 1990s (Lee 1995). What seems to be particularly important today is to take into consideration the elements of independence mentioned above and combine them with activities carried out in a way that ensures survival and "getting heard."

In the discussion so far, we have put a lot of emphasis on record labels because they were the main carriers of independence in the traditional 20th century model. Similar dilemmas and criteria can be taken into account when considering the independence of individual artists. Due to the changes taking place in the music market during the last 20 years, the analysis of the concept of independence must be gradually expanded to include analysis of individual artists. Who can be seen as an "independent artist?" Does cooperation with an independent label automatically mean that a given musician should be perceived as independent, as was the case 40 years ago?

As we mentioned in earlier chapters, when analyzing independence, we cannot forget the aspect of money. Artists have limited possibilities of functioning on a large scale in the capitalist production system if they do not take into account the rules according to which that system operates. It forces us to see the career as an object to be managed and to be matched to opportunities appearing in the music market (Haynes and Marshall 2018; Morris 2013). Therefore, contemporary discussions of independence should focus, to a larger extent, not on the opposition to major record companies (independent artists can successfully operate without their mediation) but rather on the position of artists in the face of the seemingly limitless possibilities offered by capitalism. Unlike in the 1970s, theoretically, today musicians have a greater chance to realize their artistic vision, as long as they are able to find the means to support it. By "a greater chance," we mean the availability of recording technologies, digital distribution, and direct communication with recipients. Although obtaining funds in the cultural sector has always been rather challenging, today the possibilities are greater[2] than they were in the traditional model (dominant in music in the second half of the 20th century). However, this does not automatically mean greater independence: on the one hand, the artist is not doomed to choose between financing through a record label and self-financing; on the other hand, however, she has to face the fact that she must obtain the funds for her activity (at least in the beginning) on her own. A musician investing one's own money in a precarious career is not the type of independence that is desirable.

Compared to, for example, the 1970s, the chances that a record label will spend money on an album recording are significantly smaller, while the number of entities that might replace the label is larger. Prescinding from the different situations of artists in different countries, available options may be, for example, brand sponsorship, grants distributed by government and non-governmental institutions, and crowdfunding. Each of these sources has its own specificity and, although it may not be immediately easy to notice, some of them locate artists far from the ideals of independence. A growing dependence of individual artists on brand sponsorship seems particularly to be an issue that is overlooked in discussions of contemporary understandings of independence (with the notable exceptions of Hesmondhalgh and Meier 2015 and Meier 2017). The problem with unsigned artists being sponsored by corporations outside of the music industry was particularly well put by Macio Moretti, an independent Polish multi-instrumentalist. Moretti was asked about the importance of maintaining independence, defined as not having the backing of big capital, and said the following:

> It is extremely important, but if you have a lot of crazy ideas it's difficult, unfortunately. I have a lot of extremely crazy ideas but I don't act on all of them, because I know how many compromises I would have to accept, which would not necessarily be positive. Compromises are OK if the person you compromise with has a vision, but as we know, big capital does not follow an artistic vision, just one of demand and supply. Consequently, it's a little sad that I know there are many things I won't do because I don't want to tie myself to big capital. Also, I believe it's most important to us as people to try not to be carriers of someone else's ideas that we disagree with, or to be an advertising post.
>
> (Galuszka 2020, 221)

If we follow the line of reasoning presented in this citation, we can conclude that of all methods of financing music making alternative to record labels, crowdfunding is distinguished by the fact that it is based not on "big capital" but on direct support from the audience. This draws it closest to the understanding of independence indicated by Dunn, quoted earlier (2012).

The changes taking place in the music market have generated a number of challenges that affect, to a similar degree, both small music labels and independent artists. The imbalance in the relationship between these entities and streaming platforms, such as Spotify, can serve as an example. This imbalance translates into worse cooperation conditions being offered to small entities, e.g. the inability to provide recording catalogs to streaming platforms directly. This means that, unlike major record companies, a small entity must use the mediation of a so-called music aggregator, which requires additional costs. Even if such solutions result directly from economic factors (Galuszka 2015) and not from deliberate discrimination against small entities, they pose real problems for this sector. In the context of the analysis that we are performing in this book, an important question arises: to what extent can crowdfunding become a kind of game-changer – a mechanism that, by emphasizing authenticity and a direct relationship between the initiator of the collection and the contributors, can alleviate some of the disadvantages that small players face in the music market.

Crowdfunded independent labels

Although crowdfunding is primarily perceived as a tool that gives independence to individual artists, we want to open the analysis with a less obvious question: can crowdfunding platforms function as independent record labels? To achieve that, a platform would need to adopt a certain ideological position, concentrate mostly on releasing music, and manage to achieve financial stability, i.e. survive in the market for longer than just a while. These criteria eliminate most platforms, for example Kickstarter. Although it is incorporated as a benefit corporation (Kickstarter 2015a), which makes some of its goals close to those of independent record labels, it does not release music (it is just a mechanism for collecting funds that help artists release music), and it concentrates on a much wider spectrum of creative activities than just music. Kickstarter, Indiegogo, and several other platforms may help labels and individual artists gather funds for their projects, but they are not labels themselves. This section concentrates on four other platforms that were much closer to being fan-funded independent record labels. Our analysis concentrates on the business sustainability of these ventures, and their ideological positions.

The theoretical tool that will help us analyze the business sustainability of these platforms is the business model. It denotes "the business logic of a specific firm" and describes "the value a company offers to one or several segments of customers" that generates "profitable and sustainable revenue streams" (Osterwalder et al. 2005, 17). Two key elements of a business model are methods of creating value (what benefits customers receive) and capturing value (how the company makes profits) (Kohler 2015). Naturally, independent record labels are not the main interest of business studies, particularly if we take into account that some of them want to avoid any association with "business." Nevertheless, the business model concept is useful in determining whether a new type of venture – such as a crowdfunding platform – is sustainable and can survive in the long term. Without business sustainability, independents risk following the fate of their 1990s predecessors, which either went bankrupt or were bought out (Lee 1995).

MegaTotal

MegaTotal, started in 2007 in Poland, was one of the first crowdfunding platforms in Eastern Europe. It is a prime representative of the fanvesting model (Galuszka and Bystrov 2014b). MegaTotal implemented a unique variant of this model in which contributors not only became "shareholders" in projects (i.e. were promised a share in profits if albums sold well), but which also motivated them to contribute to the projects as early as possible through a sophisticated incentivizing mechanism.[3] We wrote about MegaTotal earlier (Galuszka and Brzozowska 2016, 2017a, 2017b), and to avoid repetition we will concentrate here only on one aspect of its operations – the platform's business model. This analysis is important in the context of this book as it shows reasons why this independent "social record label" – as MegaTotal called itself – failed.

The business model of the first version of MegaTotal (until December 2011) was based on creating value for both artists and contributors. In general, artists were offered free promotional tools (a free artist profile, which enabled communication with the public and streaming music to listeners) and the possibility to gather funds for recording an album. When the platform started in 2007, a free artist profile was itself a valuable tool for most debutants, who did not have access to a wide variety of promotional websites such as are in use today. Therefore, some artists registered with the platform even if they did not count on gathering enough funds to record their music.

Listeners were offered the opportunity to contribute financial resources to projects initiated by artists in exchange for equity stakes that gave them a share in any profits earned by the record after its release (proportionate to the contributor's stake), financial bonuses thanks to the functioning of the incentivizing mechanism (Galuszka and Bystrov 2014a, 2014b), free unlimited music streams, and access to music-related content generated by the community of users and artists (e.g. news, discussions). MegaTotal positioned itself as a "social record label" (to artists) and "a place where you can earn on music", and "a place where you can discover talents and listen to your favorite music for free and legally" (to contributors).

Until December 2011 the business model implemented by MegaTotal was based on two main sources of revenue: advertising income (correlated with the number of visitors to the platform's website and the time they spent on the website – both were at that time significant), and financial interest earned on funds contributed to the projects on the platform. One of the founders of MegaTotal summarized it as follows:

> The half million zlotys that we gathered for releasing those 70 records is just the tip, and there's also the very long tail of money that was deposited on the account and held until any of the projects would be completed.
>
> (interview 2)[4]

The respondent refers to the fact that thanks to complex rules in which funds circulated among contributors, at any time there was a large number of projects that received some contributions but stopped attracting additional capital. Such projects were allowed to remain on the platform as long as their initiators wanted, while MegaTotal earned interest on the funds.

It should be noted, however, that this construction of the platform's business model, in particular the fact that MegaTotal had no financial stakes in the releases, had profound consequences for its functioning. First, when a crowdfunded album was sold on the market, MegaTotal enjoyed only indirect benefits (the platform's popularity, more projects, more contributors) – all the profits went to artists (50%) and contributors (50%). Second, MegaTotal took no risk in releasing music; all the risk was shifted to the contributors. Consequently, unlike traditional record labels, MegaTotal did not need to construct a varied portfolio of recordings to spread the risk over several titles (Caves 2000). While the lack of a stake in profits weakened the platform's chances for functioning as a record label as it gave it no money to invest in the promotion of releases, the lack of risk allowed it not to go bankrupt because of poor sales of releases. MegaTotal's founders were aware of the deficiencies of this model and decided to improve it, and the new model was finalized in January 2012.

While there were several reasons why the owners of MegaTotal decided to redesign the platform (e.g. the code and the design of the website were dated, and it was possible to get the EUA funding to finance the redesign process), the most important one was the founders' understanding that MegaTotal's methods of capturing value were not sufficient to sustain the operation of the platform in the long run. The following statement illustrates what MegaTotal's founders thought of the platform's business model in 2011:

> The reality is that we lack sufficient resources to accomplish everything. The "50-50" mechanism of dividing the contributions has its advantages – its clarity and transparency is nice and we can talk about the "fair music" rule and so on, but as I was saying, we

receive no commission on all those transactions – if we did, then perhaps our potential would be different.

(interview 1)

The problem of the lack of sufficient resources would not be so severe if MegaTotal managed to attract popular artists who could become the platform's "cash cows." This never materialized – platform's roster consisted of debutants and only a few mid-level artists. Additionally, these artists expected the platform to provide them with a level of engagement similar to one they could get from a traditional record label, while due to lack of resources all they could count on was low-cost online promotion on the platform's website and social networking sites. Artists' expectations may have been, to a certain extent, caused by mistakes made during the launch and positioning of the platform, which suggested that the platform operated like a typical record label. At a certain point it became evident that if MegaTotal wanted its artists to attain higher levels of popularity, it needed to build mechanisms for promoting them, which meant finding money to finance them.

There were also two issues on the contributors' side. First, the founders of MegaTotal wanted to solve the problem of users withdrawing their earnings from the platform. Although this was not really profitable for most of the contributors, since the withdrawal of their funds subjected them to a 23% VAT surcharge, there were some exceptionally savvy investors who managed to earn and withdraw significant sums of money from the platform. Such withdrawals harmed the very essence of MegaTotal's business model as they diminished the funds in service and consequently the financial interest such funds brought. Second, pressure from contributors forced MegaTotal to address the problem of incomplete projects, i.e. those abandoned by artists. On one hand, the funds gathered for such projects generated financial interest, which was one of the elements of MegaTotal's business model. On the other hand, however, abandoned projects frustrated contributors, who had no access to the funds they invested in such projects. Consequently, MegaTotal's founders realized that if they wanted to sustain the image of being "fair," they needed to solve that problem.

The founders of MegaTotal addressed these issues by redesigning the platform's business model, layout, and functionalities. The following changes were implemented:

1. Introduction of sales of services. Prior to January 2012, it was understood that artists who completed the gathering of funds for

their projects were, by default, guided by the platform's employees through the process of releasing a record. Following the changes introduced, after January 2012 they were given the option of releasing their records with MegaTotal or through external record labels. This meant that once an artist gathered the desired sum of money, she could either release her music with MegaTotal or use the funds to bankroll a recording session or promotional campaign with any of the record labels that were active in the recording market. If she chose the former, then MegaTotal would charge her for the services she used (e.g. designing a CD cover, filming a video), which would bring the platform money.

2. Relinquishment of profit sharing with contributors. As of January 2012, contributors were no longer promised revenue from the sale of records once the project was completed. All they could count on were the bonuses gained thanks to the incentivizing mechanism during the process of gathering funds. As mentioned, from 2012, once the project reached its goal, the artist was free to negotiate the release of a record with any label. If he chose to release it with MegaTotal, then the platform could count on revenue from the exploitation of the copyright in the sound recording. This, in theory, would give MegaTotal an incentive to invest in the promotion of the recording – a factor that was clearly missing before January 2012.

3. Opening a new version of the digital music store, where apart from buying the CDs and digital music files of the platform's artists, other musical products could also be bought. The introduction of a store was combined with a ban on the direct withdrawal of contributor funds from the platform (the only way to withdraw money was to terminate a contributor's account). The idea was that any earnings generated by contributors would be spent in MegaTotal's store, which gave the platform the possibility to generate revenues even if contributors decided to cash in their profits.

4. Building a network of stakeholders. As mentioned above, MegaTotal planned to guide an artist through the recording process by recommending recording studios, rehearsal sites, equipment manufacturers, etc. If the platform had managed to help finance several projects, then the aforementioned stakeholders would have been charged a fee for obtaining new clients from MegaTotal.

5. Introduction of time limits within which a project had to be completed. If an artist did not manage to reach her financial goal

Crowdfunding and independence in music 77

within a predefined time frame (the higher the financial goal, the more time an artist was given), then the funds invested went back to the contributors and the project started the collection phase over again. The idea was to give artists more incentive to pursue their projects actively and lead to a more efficient circulation of funds between artists and contributors while also protecting contributors from having their money tied up in dormant projects.

6. Moving towards positioning MegaTotal as a "financial mechanism to support your favorite artists." By allowing artists to choose any label to release their records, combined with the offer to sell their services, MegaTotal broke with its image of the "social record label."

7. Opening the platform to non-musical projects. The new version of the platform was not limited to music projects. From 2012, any type of cultural good could be crowdfunded – e.g. books, movies, or computer programs.

8. Introduction of the mechanism of rewards. Until January 2012, the rewards were offered only to the top 30 contributors – a free CD and a "thank you" notice printed on the CD sleeve. From January 2012, MegaTotal allowed project initiators to offer rewards similarly as was done on Kickstarter. This unfortunately generated another problem: conflict between the functioning of the incentivizing mechanism and the system of bonuses. Given the rules of the incentivizing mechanism, it should be noted that in order for a targeted level of capital to be collected, the amount of money actually paid by contributors should be almost twice as large as the target (adjusting for the first contribution), because half of the money paid by contributors was distributed among their predecessors. This meant that in practice any bonuses offered by an artist would cost contributors twice as much as in the absence of the incentivizing mechanism. Unfortunately, the only way to resolve this conflict would be to eliminate the incentivizing mechanism. MegaTotal's founders considered but never executed this, as doing so would mean losing the platform's unique features.

Despite the significant effort made by MegaTotal's employees in re-designing the platform, its users, above all the contributors, rejected the changes. In particular, depriving contributors of profits from the sale of releases and the ban on direct withdrawal of contributor funds from the platform were strongly criticized. They were seen as a breach of an implicit "contract" between the platform and its users, which emphasized "being fair." This caused a constant flow of users from the platform and led to its going dormant in 2018.

An analysis of the case of MegaTotal shows that although entering the music market with a completely new business model is feasible, making the model profitable requires great effort, business intuition, and balancing between user expectations and economic constraints. We can evaluate MegaTotal's case on two levels. The first one refers to the ideological position of the platform. As we mentioned elsewhere, MegaTotal

> highlighted the idea of being "fair" toward artists and fans on their website. The primary manifestation of this attitude was sharing the profit from sales between both parties, which to some extent constituted a reference point for the record industry, but, in contrast to independent/do-it-yourself record labels, did not result from a consistent ideology.
>
> (Galuszka and Brzozowska 2017a, 846)

Not surprisingly, when users believed that the changes implemented in 2012 were not "fair" anymore, they left the platform. These changes, however, correspond with the second level of our analysis – the business evaluation of the project. The pre-2012 version of the platform's business model had deficiencies with regard to capturing value. This was a consequence of MegaTotal's decision not to collect any commission (for instance, Kickstarter and Indiegogo charge a 5% platform fee plus payment processing fees), which resulted in the necessity to look for other, less reasonable ways of capturing value. When MegaTotal attempted to introduce new ways of capturing value in 2012, it met strong opposition from its users who saw the changes in ideological terms. The changes, reasonable from a business point of view, were unacceptable to the users and MegaTotal never found a way to regain their trust.

SellaBand, MyMajorCompany, ArtistShare

Interesting conclusions can be drawn from a comparison of the business model of MegaTotal with the models implemented by other platforms. The first that should be mentioned is the Dutch/German platform SellaBand, which was one of the pioneers of crowdfunding (detailed analyses of this platform can be found in Agrawal et al. (2015) and Ordanini et al. (2011)). SellaBand was launched in 2006 and helped more than 80 artists fund and record their albums, attracting funds estimated at over $4 million (SellaBand 2015). The platform went bankrupt for the first time in 2010 but was saved by external investors, only to go bankrupt a second time in 2015, this time permanently.

SellaBand allowed contributors to participate in profits coming from the sale of records released by the platform, which were divided equally[5] between project initiators, contributors, and the platform (Agrawal et al. 2015). From the business point of view, this was advantageous as it gave the platform money necessary to conduct its business. What went wrong then? The answer was available on SellaBand's website from the very beginning of the platform: a tiny diagram that explained what happened to $50,000 gathered by project initiators. It explained that 60% of the sum would be spent on recording the CD, 18% on printing it, and 22% on delivering it. Artists who crowdfund on Kickstarter also spend money doing these things, but in their case the approach is bottom-up – each project initiator proposes her own budget. Even if most of them need a CD, they are free to set the proportions on their own, which may mean for example lowering the recording budget. SellaBand, however, approached the business the major label way, which meant opting for expensive recording sessions that consumed 60% of the crowdfunded sum. Since the rest was spent on printing and sending the CD, no funds were left for promotion. SellaBand's business model was much simpler than that of MegaTotal; however, it was not flexible enough to accommodate to changing realities of the music market, where being noticed by the target audience is much more important than delivering music on tangible records. SellaBand presented itself as giving artists more freedom than traditional record labels. First, it emphasized that project initiators could leave the platform before raising the full amount. Today it is an industry-standard, but back then, this argument was used to position SellaBand as more artist-friendly than traditional record labels. Second, SellaBand asserted that the artist's cooperation with the platform was limited to releasing the crowdfunded album. This was presented as superior to long-term contracts offered by some record labels, which supposedly stifled creativity. According to the platform's website, this was supposed to be a breakthrough in the music industry:

> SellaBand aims to level the playing field in the global recording industry. The mission is to break the rules and change the rules, not to hold you back by creating rules. It is about getting you to

the next level and at all time you will remain in control of your own music destiny.

(SellaBand 2009)

However, by opting for expensive recording sessions, SellaBand acted unlike independent labels. Despite the narrative about "changing the rules," SellaBand was far from the anti-mainstream ideology of independents.

Another interesting platform that represented the fanvesting model was MyMajorCompany. Started in 2007 in France, it enjoyed some initial successes, which gave it significant press coverage and access to capital (both from contributors and from investors interested in investing in the company itself) in a much larger scale than in the case of MegaTotal. In its early years, MyMajorCompany divided profits from the sale of albums between the project initiator – artist (40%), contributors (40%), and the platform (20%) (Bordier 2008). Between 2010 and 2011 the platform attempted to enter with this participatory model into other cultural markets in France, which led to the opening of MyMajorCompany Books, MyMajorCompany Comics, and MyMajorCompany UK, the last of which was an attempt at expansion into the British market. None of these initiatives managed to achieve economic sustainability, and in 2012 the platform merged all these initiatives into one and redesigned itself, switching to a Kickstarter-like model. It can therefore be said that before 2012, MyMajorCompany's idea resembled MegaTotal and SellaBand with regard to giving contributors shares in the profits earned by released albums. Unlike MegaTotal, however, MyMajorCompany's revenues were directly related to the success of its releases. On the top of that, at least three of its music releases brought contributors significant revenues.[6] Nevertheless, MyMajorCompany lost money on its crowdfunding operations and managed to stay afloat thanks to its record label division (the two entities were separated) and its access to financial investors. In 2016, the company announced it was ending the funding of new projects and concentrated on other initiatives, among them, running regular record labels.

The most fascinating aspect of the functioning of MyMajorCompany is that at least three of its releases brought contributors significant profits (Nedmic 2012). Although, taking into account that the platform released a few dozen albums, this number may seem small, this proportion resembles the success rates of traditional record labels, estimated to be on average between about 10% and 20% (i.e. 10% to 20% of releases bring profits, which offset losses generated by the rest (Papadopoulos 2004)). Unlike traditional record labels, however, MyMajorCompany had to share the revenues with contributors. On the other hand, it did not bear the risk as, contrary to a traditional record label, it did not invest its own but rather contributor money. Nevertheless, this model turned out to be unsustainable in the long run.

We would also like to address another question: how did MyMajorCompany manage to achieve significant success with some of their releases (e.g. the first album by Grégoire, which reached the top of the French sales chart)? Taking into account that the majority of MegaTotal's and SellaBand's artists struggled to gain any recognition, selling a huge number of records in one of the largest European markets is impressive. Rouzé explains it by paying attention to the fact that MyMajorCompany from its start had close ties with the French division of one of the music majors – Warner, "which handled its publishing and distribution" (2019, 45). Regarding the market triumph of Grégoire, Matthews et al. note that "the success of that particular campaign (and the 'expectations' in terms of the funds that could be raised) had been carefully prepared and orchestrated by the platform MyMajorCompany well ahead of its launch, in particular by signing a publishing contract beforehand with the distributor Warner Music France" (2019, 86). This suggests that MyMajorCompany was indeed very different from MegaTotal, which never had any ties with major record companies. Close ties with Warner and a mainstream music repertoire do not look like features of an independent record label. On the other hand, taking into account that MyMajorCompany's artists received 40% of profits from album sales, the success of some of its releases brought musicians good money. It constitutes a step in the direction of fairer fund distribution rules, which is one of the main postulates of independents.

ArtistShare is considered the first crowdfunding platform. It launched its first project in 2003. ArtistShare has drawn significant news media and industry attention, with several Grammy Awards and nominations received by its artists. ArtistShare is similar to the three platforms mentioned above in its attempts at building a comprehensive business model that can be perceived as an alternative to a traditional record label. Actually, its founder – Brian Camelio – talks of the platform as a label that "looks after the entire project from initial artistic concept through to production, distribution and marketing. The other platforms focus only on the funding aspect. After this the artist is on their own" (Read 2020). Unlike the three platforms discussed above, ArtistShare built a sustainable model and continues to release music. Let us have a look at the sources of their success.

First, ArtistShare concentrates on relatively few artists and maintains a stable repertoire policy through releasing mostly jazz records. Unlike platforms that allow any artist to crowdfund, it actively shapes its repertoire policy through curatorial decisions aimed at eliminating candidates that do not fit platform's profile. Thanks to specialization, the platform can keep promotion costs lower as it does not have to chase mainstream listeners, which is expensive. Additionally, jazz listeners are on average relatively affluent, which means they may have higher disposable income that can be spent on supporting crowdfunded artists (Veenstra 2015).

Second, ArtistsShare does not make attempts at building a model that remunerates contributors with part of the revenue from selling crowdfunded albums. The source of the platform's income is commission, which is negotiated individually with artists. According to one source, artists can keep up to 80% of revenues, although how exactly this number is calculated is not revealed (Williams and Wilson 2016). On the top of this, artists retain copyright of recordings, which is particularly attractive from their point of view (Thorley 2012). This makes ArtistShare close to the ideals of music independence.

Third, ArtistShare works closely with artists. This is a consequence of its repertoire policy, but it also has significant business consequences. Thanks to avoiding a one-size-fits-all approach, it can better respond to artists' needs and together with them build promotional strategies.

Fourth, ArtistShare cooperates most of all with artists that have some history on the music scene. They usually have a fan base, which makes it easier to collect donations and helps reduce promotion costs (Thorley 2012).

Summing up, it can be said that out of a few models for building crowdfunded record labels, the one implemented by ArtistShare has proved to be the most realistic. Perhaps its most interesting feature is that of all the platforms discussed in this section, ArtistShare is most reminiscent of traditional record labels. It is different because of its implementing crowdfunding mechanisms to collect funds, but the rest of its operations resemble regular record label work. While this model has advantages over the sophisticated mechanisms proposed by MegaTotal, SellaBand, and MyMajorCompany, ArtistShare's success is limited by its specialization and size. It is possible that building a large crowdfunded independent record label is a too difficult and risky venture and, therefore, music crowdfunding remains dominated by Kickstarter, Patreon, and their clones, which are not labels but mechanisms for collecting money.

Crowdfunded independent musicians

As mentioned above, crowdfunding is seen as a tool that brings independence to individual artists. Taking into account that, as we emphasized earlier, there are many types of crowdfunding as well as many types of creative projects requiring different forms of financing, it is difficult to propose generalizations concerning what is good for all musicians. Instead, in this section, we would like to show the costs that come with using crowdfunding to finance independent artists. Our analysis shows that while crowdfunding has emancipatory potential, it brings new challenges for those who decide to use it.

The problem of accountability

Before the advent of the internet and all the changes it brought to the music business, listeners rarely had deep insights into the costs of releasing an album or the profits it brought. The public was aware of the earnings of top stars because this topic was attractive for mainstream media. The existence of masses of under-waged artist received less media attention, so images of the economic attractiveness of being a pop musician were generally biased. The internet gave the public access to more information on the challenges faced by musicians, through popularization of analyses written earlier (e.g. Steve Albini's "The Problem with Music" (Albini 1993), which showed how unfavorable to musicians were the contracts they signed with big labels) to more recent stories on how major record labels were unresponsive to artists' needs (Peirson-Hagger 2020). In a way, money was a topic present even in very principled DIY circles – when in the 1970s Crass proposed a policy of selling records as inexpensively as possible ("pay no more than …"), they also addressed this issue (Gosling 2004). Crowdfunding, however, brought financial aspects of independent artists' careers to the fore. It adds a new dimension to relationships between artists and their audiences.

As was mentioned before, anti-commercialism (Marshall 2005), not emphasizing profit-maximization (Dunn 2012), and responsibility to oneself and not to a bank balance (Moore 2002) are essential elements of how being an independent artist is understood. While this does not preclude asking for donations on crowdfunding platforms, it may be a source of potential tensions as artist may easily be accused of "asking too much" or "spending the money the wrong way." This is just one step from being seen as a "commercial," "for profit," or "mainstream" artist.

The example of Amanda Palmer discussed in the introduction shows the vulnerable position in which a successful crowdfunding campaign places an independent artist. In her case, the value of contributions she received from backers: $1,192,793 – more than ten times the goal she set for her campaign ($100,000), made questions about the way she spent the funds seem justified (Kickstarter 2018). Some less oriented observers may have been puzzled when she said that "[t]he dirty secret of my Kickstarter is that it was actually a loss leader leading to Patreon"[7] (O'Malley Greenburg 2015, n.p.). Even before making this statement, she had posted on her campaign page on Kickstarter a detailed explanation of how she had spent the money (Kickstarter 2012). In fact, she also admitted elsewhere that her campaign on Kickstarter was poorly budgeted (Hurst 2016). Her subsequent successes on Patreon prove that she managed to convince her audience that her management of the finances was "fair and square." Nevertheless, when the artist engages in asking for donations and subsequent direct discussion about money with the audience, she opens the floor to more personal and at times unfair or even ridiculous questions. In 2015, Palmer revealed she had received an email in which a fan, "Worried-but-Still-Devoted," questioned her reasons for joining Patreon. Although the letter starts with expressions of admiration, it is written in an accusatory style. The point taken by the author boils down to arguing that there was no coincidence in Palmer announcing her pregnancy shortly after joining Patreon and that motherhood will affect the quality of her work:

> Are your patrons paying for new music, or are they paying for a new baby? (…) Bottom line is, I need answers before I can feel comfortable giving you more of the money that I earned with my own sweat and tears.
>
> (Palmer 2015, n.p.)

It is easy to dismiss such accusations as only a slightly camouflaged form of trolling; however, let us treat this as just another way of asking about the limits of artistic independence. In other words: is a crowdfunded independent artist free to use donations any way he or she wants? The question is complex, and the answer requires asking a different question: does the artist deliver rewards as promised? By "rewards" we mean anything that is the artist's part of the bargain: CDs that should be delivered to contributors' private addresses, songs that should be written and circulated among contributors, meetings with fans, etc. If yes, then all else is a matter of communication between an artist and her fans. It can be assumed that such communication will appear differently with various artists, depending on their decisions, fans' expectations, and conventions accepted in a given genre of music. In the long term, it is fairly easy to evaluate what works: numbers of patrons and their declared monthly contributions either increase or fall. Naturally, not all such fluctuations may be explained by accountability, as they may very well be caused by changes in the quality of music that an artist delivers. Nevertheless, an artist who chose a certain mode of communication with patrons, e.g. full transparency, receives feedback from them, and in that context should interpret falling or increasing numbers of contributions.

Let us return to the email Amanda Palmer received from fan "Worried-but-Still-Devoted." Her answer seems to correspond with our line of reasoning presented above:

> But honestly? Why shouldn't they buy baby formula with that money? It's just there on the list of stuff they need to survive on tour, up there with everything else like gas, food, and capital to print t-shirts. It would be a like a diabetic singer promising her fans that she wasn't going to spend her Kickstarter tour money on insulin.
>
> (Palmer 2015, n.p.)

Even if we agree that Palmer's arguments are self-explanatory, the fact that she commented on the email shows that while crowdfunded independence gives freedom, it also brings new, unpleasant duties that cost artists time and emotional engagement. Additionally, it is difficult to miss the gender aspect of the email. It is rather unlikely that a male artist receives such comments from his listeners, not only because fatherhood is less physically demanding, at least in the beginning, but also because probably no one would look for any correlation between the decision to join Patreon and becoming a father. Palmer's answer shows that "Worried-but-Still-Devoted" touched a chord – she called it a "pregnant artist's worst nightmare to get a letter like this" (Palmer 2015, n.p.). Crowdfunding and other social media have exposed aspects of artists' lives that in previous decades would not have been discussed with listeners. Thirty years ago, for example, fans probably would not have written letters to Palmer to express their doubts about signing a deal with an independent record label immediately after becoming pregnant.

Another powerful example of problems faced by independent musicians who use crowdfunding comes from the aforementioned Polish platform, MegaTotal. Let us analyze a discussion between a contributor and a band that took place in platform's forum (now inactive) in 2010. A user of the site started a thread concerning the fact that one of the bands had begun raising funds for the release of a second album despite the low sales of the first album:

> According to official data, the band managed to sell 26 copies of its first album, including 17 copies for the special price of 6.99 PLN. So from the contributed 5000 PLN [...] about 44.96 PLN was returned to the fans/investors. This gives an investment return of −99.1%. Great deal: we gave 5000 PLN and got less than 50 PLN, and they are going to ask for more soon. This is either a joke or blatant mockery. Do you take us for idiots, losers, and suckers?

The rest of this rather long post lists how much money its author put into the production of the first album, how this relates to his monthly income, and how disappointed he is with the whole situation.

The statements quoted above received a reply from the band, who frustrated many users of the forum with their decision to start a new fundraising campaign for a second album. This reply reveals the band's hesitation whether to crowdfund the new album and understanding of fans' frustrations. The band asks to be judged on the quality of music and not their marketing skills. It also shows discomfort felt by the artist when asking for donations:

> Writing these couple of sentences, I'm also filled with distaste, because I would like to create art, and at this moment I feel as if I were a salesman and I had to make excuses to my superior about an unfulfilled sales plan.

This discussion shows that the model of crowdfunding proposed by MegaTotal, in which the fans contribute to the costs of releasing an album but are at the same time given profits from its sales, leads to attempts at holding artists accountable for the success of the common undertaking. While fans in the traditional, pre-internet model of music production and distribution cared about an artist's success, which could translate into wishing them high sales for their recordings, in the model proposed by MegaTotal, the relationship between the parties obtained a financial character. The strength of the financial relationship and, therefore, the pressure to achieve high sales, depended on whether a given contributor identified themselves as a fan of the artist (which is why they supported the artist's project financially), considered themselves an investor, or combined both motivations (Galuszka and Bystrov 2014b). Regardless of the fact that fans in the past (in the traditional model) could expect from an artist a certain level of engagement in the promotion of the recording, the addition of financial motivations has particular consequences for the mutual relationship, as the presented discussion shows.

This is a rather extreme example, as it involved discussion about potential profits. Nevertheless, even the example of Amanda Palmer's troubles presented earlier, where no potential profits for contributors were envisaged, shows that the artist's accountability is of primary importance in crowdfunding. Thirty years ago, if fans had doubts whether an artist is a "real independent," they would have asked the artist if she was selling out. In the case of a crowdfunded artists today they can do this too – plus, they can raise other issues related to the ways in which their contributions are used.

Independence as rhetorical argument

Independence, even though, as we argued earlier, the meaning of this term has blurred, continues to be a powerful concept used by many project initiators as a rhetorical argument aimed at attracting donations. In a way it is nothing new – "independence is a central rhetorical means for legitimation purposes for various types of media in different contexts" (Karppinen and Moe 2016, 112). When a TV or a radio station wants to emphasize its independence, for example with the purpose of gaining credibility, it takes from this concept what suits them, arguing that either the private or the public sector guarantees more independence. Not surprisingly, artists who crowdfund their projects also want to use the rhetorical power of independence. This comes in many variations, ranging from purely informative ("we have no affiliation with a label") through aimed at making distinctions ("we're proudly independent"), to designed to drum up sympathy ("labels ripped us off, so we're trying the indie way now"). This section discusses four campaigns on Kickstarter that, despite representing different music genres, all referred to the concept of independence. We are particularly interested in differences in the understanding, presenting, and using of the concept of independence in these campaigns.

One often used narrative relates to the freedom guaranteed by independence. In 2012, American emo pop band Allstar Weekend attracted 1,312 backers who pledged $96,262 for a $30,000 goal (Kickstarter 2013a). The campaign page contained the lead, "We've done everything with our fans so far, so this is the next natural step! Help us fund & promote our brand new album independently!"

(Kickstarter 2013a), which suggests the existence of a direct link between the band and the audience – often emphasized by artists aiming to be perceived as authentic. The description of the campaign included the following statement:

> It's the sound we want, the songs we want, the vibe we want – pretty much the first record we're making that's 100% what WE want. This time around we are making this record completely on our own, meaning we have no official record label, and no one telling us (or strongly suggesting) who we should write and record with, or what "direction" our songs should go in.
> (Kickstarter 2013a)

This could have been written by many artists who were not entirely happy with the way in which their labels handled their careers, and also by artists perceived as independent. A quick look at the history of Allstar Weekend suggests that this is a rather frank request and, at the same time, that the band is very far from being "independent" or "authentic" according to the criteria listed by Dunn (2012) or Marshall (2005). The band was formed by a group of high school friends in 2007 and gained popularity in 2009 thanks to Radio Disney's contest the Next Big Thing. Shortly after, they signed a contract with Hollywood Records – a label of Disney Music Group. Allstar Weekend recorded two albums (which peaked at 197 and 49 on the Billboard 200) and a couple of shorter records for this label. On the 9th of January 2012 – a few months before initiating the Kickstarter campaign – the following statement was published on the band's website:

> We asked Hollywood Records to let us go and they were very awesome about it. Just because they didn't want our vision, doesn't mean they didn't understand it. We thank everyone there for believing in us and giving us our first big break. There is no bad blood between us and the label, and we weren't dropped.
> (Allstar Weekend 2012)

Shortly after, the band run a successful Kickstarter campaign and disbanded. The crowdfunded record was released under a new name – The Tragic Thrills (Kickstarter, 2013b). The new band's self-titled album was not as successful as earlier Allstar Weekend releases.

This case is particularly interesting if we look at it taking into account that independence is "often a relative quality rather than one that entails absolute or clear-cut distinctions between one thing and another" (King 2015, 52). Allstar Weekend was not an independent band, and when it started its Kickstarter campaign it capitalized on a fanbase built during their contract with Hollywood Records – an opposite of what we could call an independent label. Nevertheless, they used the narrative of independence in their campaign and, taking into account their earlier position, it was certainly a move towards being more independent. If Allstar Weekend was still signed to Hollywood Records, they would not have needed to seek crowdfunding money, but they would have had to accept at least some of label's proposals regarding their image and music. For contributors who knew the band's history, this constituted a logical whole – with that campaign, the band was becoming more independent. For academics who study the concept of music independence, this may be a bit more complicated, as Allstar Weekend is very far from how independence is understood in popular music studies (see the first part of this chapter). It cannot, however, be denied that Kickstarter helped the band emancipate.

Another example of using the concept of independence to mobilize donations is the campaign of the electro-pop duo The Limousines. The group was started in 2007 and in July 2010 independently released their first album, Get Sharp. In December of the same year, the band signed a deal with the independent label Dangerbird Records. The following is how one of the band's members – Giovanni Giusti – spoke of the deal in an interview published on 23 August 2011:

> They're an an [sic!] independent label, a small group of people – they have a lot of pull, I respect all their artists. (…) There were a lot of other sharks swimming around, other labels, but the deal was good and we selected them.
>
> (Hilburn 2011)

Unfortunately, the reality proved to be more complicated, and a few months later The Limousines left the label. Several years later, the other band member described the deal they had with Dangerbird as "disastrous" (Patreon 2020).

After these experiences, Kickstarter – which at that time received significant media attention – seemed the obvious choice. The band announced they wanted to crowdfund their second full length album, "Hush." The campaign was conducted on Kickstarter in 2012 and engaged 1,767 backers who pledged $75,808 to the $30,000 goal (Kickstarter 2015c). Their project page briefly described their story, emphasizing bad experiences they had when cooperating with a record label. The narrative does not make any distinction between "evil majors" and "good independents" – here, all labels are "evil":

> we could easily get another record deal, but that would just mean putting our band, our lives, in the hands of people who are less passionate about our music than we are ... people who are so worried about keeping their own jobs that they couldn't possibly have our best interests in mind, much less encourage us to be artistically adventurous.
>
> (Kickstarter 2015c)

This is supported by the band's testimony, which lists their former label's mistakes and faults. The list is rather long and includes not promoting the band's music or supporting music videos and touring financially, and severe physical and digital distribution flaws. On top of that, the band emphasizes that even though the recording and release of the album had been self-financed by The Limousines before signing Dangerbird, the label would own the rights to the recording for the next 14 years (Kickstarter 2015c).

We do not know the label's version of this story, and we should seriously consider the possibility that it may have failed the band's hopes in certain areas, such as the distribution of CDs. We should also assume that the band, being the weaker party in the contractual relationship, could not afford to take legal actions against the label for a breach of contract. It is particularly unfortunate that the band licensed the label for so many years songs that were recorded before signing the deal, which meant divesting themselves of their most valuable asset. We can only guess that this was the condition under which the label agreed to sign a deal, and if this was the case the band should have considered it a clear warning bell. Nevertheless, it is doubtful that the band did not know what type of contract they had signed. The use of this information on a Kickstarter project page is therefore a rhetorical figure aimed at drumming up sympathy and, perhaps, also angering fans. This corresponds well to contributor motivations such as "Help Others" and "Support a Cause" (Gerber and Hui 2013, 14–17). The narrative that describes the whole recording business as bad, majors and independents alike, serves to accommodate exactly these motivations.

A third example of using independence to frame the process of gathering funds is a campaign by the rapper known by the stage name Lil Dicky. His career is a spectacular example of a well-planned, entrepreneurial approach to building a stage personality, characterized by perfect timing and the ability to avoid significant mistakes (Berkowitz 2015). In 2013, he started regularly releasing his songs on YouTube, one per week for five months. Some of them came with music videos which, despite being low-cost, were praised for their adroitness. He clearly used his experience of working in the advertising business and knowledge he gained during his studies at the University of Richmond, where he pursued a marketing degree. In November 2013, he initiated a campaign to fund the recording of his album, music videos, and touring. The campaign was a huge success supported by 2,813 backers who pledged $113,017 for the $70,000 goal (Kickstarter 2015b). This success would not have materialized if Lil Dicky had not earlier built a solid fan base on YouTube and other social media. Let us analyze a short excerpt from his Kickstarter campaign page:

> And to maintain complete creative control, I REALLY want to avoiding aligning myself with a company (ie a record label) that would restrict me, both creatively and financially. Once someone else is calling the shots, it can really inhibit the artist. In looking at my work, you'll see it isn't necessarily "corporate-friendly" content.
>
> I want to create things without feeling handcuffed by a larger company. I want to make social commentary, politically incorrect statements, and absurd jokes, because that's who I am.
> (Kickstarter 2015b)

These two paragraphs are followed by a picture of hands – supposedly his – in shackles, captioned with "How can I rap and dance if I'm in shackles?" (Kickstarter 2015b). Clearly, he made no distinction between major and independent record labels; all "creative control" is presented as restrictive. Unlike "ideal-type" independent artists, anti-commercialism or a desire not to emphasize profit-maximization are not his motivations. His Kickstarter page emphasizes only the necessity of avoiding the recording business to maintain creative control. His interviews also show a purely entrepreneurial approach:

> The money is a complete necessity. To do this full time, I had to quit my job about six months ago – and I've got very little income coming in. On top of that, I spent my life's savings on the first wave of stuff, so I was at the point where I couldn't continue

without more money. But Kickstarter has been a part of my plan since day one.

(Trampe 2014)

His career after the Kickstarter campaign was hugely successful. The album recorded thanks to the Kickstarter campaign reached the seventh position on the Billboard 200. Even though technically his album was an independent release, the development of Lil Dicky's career (e.g. releasing a single that features Ariana Grande, Justin Bieber, Ed Sheeran, and Shawn Mendes) shows a clear desire to be a mainstream artist. Lil Dicky's case is puzzling when we compare his close relationship with the mainstream with his skeptical (at least at the beginning of his career) attitude towards cooperation with traditional record labels. His case can be called entrepreneurial independence, where being independent is an element of a precisely planned business strategy.

Compared to the three campaigns discussed earlier, the one by punk rock 'n' roll band The Scurvies is rather low profile. The band was formed in 2003 in Fairbanks, Alaska, and before the Kickstarter campaign released one album (in 2007) and took part in several tours in North America (New Release Today 2011). In 2011, the band collected $8,080 for an $8,000 goal thanks to support from 92 backers (Kickstarter 2011). Not only did the band aim to gather a much smaller sum than the aforementioned campaigns, but the campaign page was also rather minimal – it contained only two updates, and no comments from contributors (compare this with, e.g. The Limousines: 59 updates, 204 comments). The main campaign page included the following description:

> The Scurvies, America's favorite high-energy fun-punk rock 'n' roll band are recording a new album to be released on their very own label and need YOUR help! For the last 7 years, The Scurvies have worked hard with a D.I.Y. ethic to bring you the very best, high quality music both on stage and through your home audio device [...] but the best thing is that once the record is funded and recorded, it'll be totally FREE to download from our website.

Contrary to the three campaigns discussed earlier in this section, this one refers directly to the DIY ethic. This is strengthened by a declaration that the crowdfunded album will be available as a free download, which should be read as "we are here not to get rich." This campaign was about collecting donations from a small, dedicated group of fans spread throughout various geographical locations. Kickstarter suited this purpose well as the mechanism for gathering pledges, but promotion of the campaign and discussion about it took place elsewhere – on forums and social media used by punk rock fans.

Is the campaign by The Scurvies more "independent" than the three campaigns previously discussed? If we take into account definitions of independence prevalent in popular music studies, then the answer is yes. All these campaigns used independence as rhetorical argument, but each of them meant something different. Although the campaign by The Limousines emphasized the band's anger at the music business, and the campaign by Lil Dickey was motivated by the desire to avoid corporate control, only The Scurvies seemed to openly declare that they are not driven by profit-maximization – at least this is how we can interpret their willingness to distribute the album as a free download.

This does not mean that the other campaigns were not conducted by artists who had independence as their goal. The point is that in each case they defined independence differently. Allstar Weekend, whose image was rather tightly controlled by the label, aimed at gaining more freedom in this respect. They capitalized on the fanbase built during their cooperation with Disney Music Group to successfully crowdfund a new record but disbanded afterward. The Limousines, who had built their career rather independently, signed with the label so that their career could gather pace only to learn that they became worse off. Leaving the label and crowdfunding represented their return to independently managing their business, but their doing so has not brought them much more fame. Lil Dickey had a precise business plan that indicated crowdfunding was a better option than seeking a record label deal. If he could reach his career goals more quickly or easily with a label or non-music business corporate sponsor, he would probably choose to do so. The great commercial success of his crowdfunded release shows that his path was the right one.

In these three cases, crowdfunding gave the artists alternatives to traditional music business ways of doing things, which is emancipatory. If, however, small details had been different – the label gave more freedom to Allstar Weekend or treated The Limousines more seriously – they would not have needed to be "independent" and crowdfund their albums. For The Scurvies, on the other hand, crowdfunding seemed the only way to release music without investing their own money in the process. Thanks to the collective effort of their fans, they were able to record an album and distribute it as a free download. This forms a coherent ideological stance that corresponds to DIY ethics, as advertised on their campaign page.

Although this analysis is by no means comprehensive, it shows that future research should further develop Dale's (2008) distinction between DIY independence and other types of independence. Our proposal is to think seriously about entrepreneurial independence (see also Dumbreck and McPherson 2015; Haynes and Marshall 2018) – a type of independence that acknowledges the necessity to master tools offered by digital capitalism in such a way that artists can flourish without cooperating with businesses that limit their artistic creativity. Crowdfunding can be such a tool, although, as we argued earlier in this book, it is also limiting in some respects. It is certainly difficult to successfully crowdfund music without deeply engaging in relational labor, understood as maintaining comprehensive, often intimate artist-fan relationships (Baym 2018). Not only is it time-consuming, but it also requires skills that some artists do not have.

Notes

1 Of course, most of the rights that have been mentioned existed in the second half it the 20th century, but their economic significance was lesser than today.
2 Greater, when it comes to the number of potentially available sources. For example, if one wants to finance the recording of their album, this can be done more cheaply today than in the 1960s, and the funds can be obtained from several sources, alternative to a record label. However, when we take into account chances that the invested funds would translate to success as measured by the number of recordings sold or the recognizability/popularity of an artist, the situation of today's artists is more difficult than that of those in the second half of the 20th century. This is due to greater competition – the number of artists pursuing the audience's attendance (Hracs et al. 2013).
3 This incentivizing mechanism can be explained as follows. Suppose that an artist wants to collect the sum of 10,000 PLN. The price of the shares in this album is the same for all contributors, with the exception of the first one. The first contributor to an album purchases the share at a nominal value, which is calculated as 50% of the amount paid in – i.e. if the contributed amount is equal to 100 PLN, then the contributor receives 50 PLN of the nominal share. The other half of the payment is used to create a 50 PLN nominal share that is owned by the artist. If the project succeeds and the capital stock of 10,000 PLN is accumulated, then the first investment of 100 PLN guarantees a share in profits from sales of the album equal to 0.5%. Each successive contributor gives away 50% of his/her payment as "dividends" to predecessors. The remaining 50% is divided equally between the contributor and the artist. Thus, the nominal value of the share that the subsequent investor receives is equal to 25% of the amount contributed – i.e. if she contributes a total of 100 PLN to the targeted 10,000 PLN, then she will receive 0.25% of the profits once the album succeeds (see also Galuszka and Bystrov 2014a, 2014b). We would like to thank Victor Bystrov for formulating it this way.

4 Three in-depth interviews with MegaTotal founders were conducted (Mariusz Dróżdż and Aleksander Pawlak, interviews 1 and 2 respectively) on 28 October 2011 and on 12 June 2013 (Aleksander Pawlak, interview 3).
5 Other source suggests different division of funds which assigned SellaBand 15% of the budget (Taylor 2015).
6 Although it is difficult to verify the numbers, one source states that the most successful project generated a return of 220% (Nedmic 2012).
7 By which she meant that she found the patronage model offered by Patreon much better for funding independent artists. Nevertheless, claiming that her record campaign at Kickstarter had been "a loss leader" may have been puzzling to some.

5 Conclusions

In the examples analyzed in this book, we wanted to present how differently the discourse of independence is implemented in crowdfunding campaigns in relation to music and film productions. We are aware that this, obviously, does not exhaust the possibilities, and the addition of another area of creativity, e.g. video games, would probably allow the identification of other problems related to the issues discussed because it would reveal how ideas about independence generated in a completely different context are transformed. However, we decided that these two areas are most closely related to the canonical portrayal of the independent artist in pop culture, and, at the same time, they allow showing diversity in ways of implementing and using new practices in the financing of culture. This allowed us to show the many various ways crowdfunding can be employed in the realm of creative industries while still remaining a phenomenon that is not fully understood (also by the artists themselves, for example, Zach Braff) and sometimes also leading to controversy (Amanda Palmer). Assuming that the issues presented here may become the basis for further research, we intended to point to the key problem, which is the need to reformulate the traditional understanding of independence because, in the case of crowdfunding seen as an umbrella term, this concept can manifest itself in a variety of ways and can become even more blurred. What is more, being aware of some utopian aspects of independence rhetoric, we wanted to point out the dangers that arise from overly literal understanding or misunderstanding of the concept. Taking into account the experience of film and music industry researchers, we have pointed out that these are not new problems; however, we are convinced that they are becoming intensified with the further introduction of the social media context and online cooperation. From this perspective, crowdfunding describes a set of functions in the relationship between the artist and the audience, while independence, as conceived by the artist, is not limited to financing but also deals with various aspects of the discourse on independence. These aspects cover both the material and the emotional sphere because they both shape relationships with fans and allow the building of emotional capital (Jenkins 2006), which is the key element of the digital economy.

Therefore, we intended to attach special importance to the fact that, in the new model, the artist must be both an entrepreneur and a manager because she is deprived of or obtains only limited support from institutions such as a label or studio. Even if such support exists, for example in the form of distribution and promotion, it does not relieve the artist from the responsibility to keep her promises or the need to communicate with contributors. This is a key issue because everything that takes place as part of crowdfunded cinema or music is subjected to communal evaluation. There, a new dimension of independent creativity is realized. Understanding this fact is crucial for creators, although, as we have seen, this understanding is not always on display. Artists themselves are also becoming more aware of this fact. For example, a documentary filmmaker, Heidi Ewing, noted that filmmakers need to change their attitudes and take responsibility for their projects (Voynar 2012). The need to rethink a promotion strategy does not mean, however, "selling yourself"; it shows that an artist understands that art also has a "business" aspect but that this does not mean that he is giving up his independence. Accepting this fact does not preclude creative freedom in the new model, in which the artist controls his piece of work along with the subsequent stages of its circulation but that at the same time gives some power to the recipients, appealing to them first and directly. This appeal, however, cannot have the character of an empty rhetorical gesture – it must have consequence in the form of a permanent mutual relation. Thus, managing one's project also means managing emotional capital, which is built in the course of mutual exchange between the creator and his fans. This unfortunately involves also costs on the artist's side, as the case of Amanda Palmer shows. Even if an independent artist shows the entrepreneurial attitudes necessary to run crowdfunding campaigns and is great in communicating with the audience, occasionally she will make a mistake or be subjected to unfair attacks by frustrated contributors. The emotional costs of crowdfunding should be investigated in future research, perhaps even more so than the skills required to succeed in fundraising.

Crowdfunding leads to a transformation of relationships between artists and audiences, and this transformation includes new risks. This clearly shows that artists are not independent in an absolute way and, what is more, they are influenced not only by the will of the founding community but also by the context of the specific community of creators. This allows us to take the discourse on independence to a slightly different level. Furthermore, in this arrangement, the new discourse on independence forces artists to take on the burden of duties that previously rested with labels. In other words, as shown by the examples in the areas of music and film that we analyzed, crowdfunding has also become a model for the promotion and distribution of independent creativity or creativity distributed independently.

In this scheme of things, one of the functions that the crowdfunding platform performs is a marketing function, which allows the "launch" of the promotion of the film or music and builds a community of recipients around it, and, as a consequence, builds the emotional capital that may allow the development of future projects. Therefore, it is not about withdrawing completely from the function that the label has performed so far but about building a network of relationships, and it is important that the network also include other artists. As numerous studies have shown, the friends and family of artists have a significant share in crowdfunding campaigns (e.g. Leibovitz et al. 2015; Ordanini et al. 2011). It is through them that the building of niche audiences often begins, which, thanks to functioning within the framework of the culture of sharing content and word-of-mouth, expands its boundaries beyond the framework available to analogous independent projects in the past. Artists should learn to fill the void caused by the absence of a studio or a label with active management of relationships with the audience, something which has been referred to as relational labor (Baym 2018).

Of course, in many cases crowdfunding, especially in film, is not able to fully replace the activities of labels and large distributors and cover the entire project budget. Certainly, it works well as an element supporting distribution and promotion, for instance through the use of word-of-mouth and the community-understood idea of "sharing" as a binder. This phenomenon is probably even more visible in the case of music, where "sharing" has numerous associations, especially in the era of internet development. It should be noted, as done by Jenkins and others (2013, 235), that participatory culture, which is based on sharing, supports the interests of independent artists and small labels. This is because, not having large budgets for advertising and distribution, they can refer to grassroots participation fans and potential fans who reach them thanks to the specifics of content sharing on social media.

Unfortunately, some artists may find crowdfunding problematic, and they have very good reasons for being skeptical. Although in both music and film digitization has brought changes that temporarily weakened the strength of major entities, it has not eliminated the economic mechanisms behind inequalities in the cultural market. For example, in the first decade of the 21st century, the position of major record companies weakened, but as soon as the next decade we could notice the reversal of this trend. Major record companies have become investors in streaming platforms, gaining something that they did not have for most of the 20th century – an impact, albeit not direct, on the final level of the music distribution channel. However, even if we ignore these moves of global corporations, it should be noted that the economic features of cultural markets (e.g. winner-take-all markets) result in the structural advantage of large entities (Caves 2003; Hesmondhalgh 2019). This can be illustrated by numerous examples, starting from the fact that major record companies can provide their record catalogs to streaming platforms incurring lower costs than independent artists (Galuszka 2015) and with much deeper pockets, resulting in potentially higher expenditure on promotion. Given that a significant proportion of recipients has no need or motivation to independently select recordings or movies, they will utilize what is most popular or is proposed by an algorithm (which may favor mainstream products of large corporations). Taking this point of view, it can be seen that the funds collected by an artist on a crowdfunding platform make it easier for him to enter the cultural production system without intermediaries in the form of record companies, and film studios, but they may not be sufficient to let him compete with these entities on equal terms. Successful use of crowdfunding seems to be more probable in the case of artists who already have a fanbase, built for example in cooperation with labels and studios. Occasional successes of individuals without any experience of cooperation with labels, as Lil Dicky's case shows, are not pure luck but result from the execution of a precise plan of building the audience by artists with business acumen.

This raises a question as to whether artists who debuted independently thanks to contributions gathered on crowdfunding platforms will choose to remain in the crowdfunding ecosystem or will make attempts to "jump" to the mainstream system of production governed by the majors. It is important to note that crowdfunding does not offer a self-sufficient, all-encompassing alternative to the ways in which culture is financed in capitalism. It is a remarkable, yet not perfect, improvement at the early phases of the production system for debutants; way of returning to the market for dropouts from systems (e.g. former stars); means to develop niche projects (such as crowdfunded independent labels); and alternative way of doing things for entrepreneurial individuals with a large following (like Amanda Palmer and Lil Dicky). While all these groups can find crowdfunding to be a useful alternative to investing their own money or to seeking brand or label sponsorship, it is particularly appealing most of all to entrepreneurial individuals with a large – or growing – following. We would like to emphasize the word "entrepreneurial" as efficient, long-term use of crowdfunding platforms, especially those functioning in the patronage model, requires a certain type of skills and personality, which makes this model suitable only for some artists. This attitude, which we propose to call "entrepreneurial independence," should be investigated in future research (see also Dumbreck and McPherson 2015; Haynes and Marshall 2018).

Here, however, the most important thing is to notice the changing context of independent creativity, which does not allow us to easily compare, for example, the first Smith's films from the 1990s with the contemporary situation of young artists seeking to be recognized on the internet. As we have seen in examples from both film and music, crowdfunding understood as a set of relationship functions is an extremely complex phenomenon. Both in the example of a typically "fan-supported" Troma and in the example of the Polish documentary *Tylko nie mów nikomu* (*Tell No One*), it was clear that the boundaries between creators and recipients are blurred. Collaboration is actually becoming co-creation, which does not mean, however, that the creator loses his authority. In the case of Troma, Lloyd Kaufman acts as a kind of a mentor who advises young filmmakers; however, their works are published next to Troma's materials, and fans have the opportunity to appear in their beloved films, which allows them to see a common context. Sekielski regards his contributors as partners in the discussion and expands the field of activity to an exclusive social media group on a crowdfunding platform. The community recognizes him as a journalistic authority and therefore builds discussions and develops its own activities around him. This goes far beyond the crowdfunding situation in which fans expect to receive rewards and end the relationship after a given campaign ends. As the example of Zach Braff showed, this ending of a relationship may also be brought about by disappointment due to not receiving the "ordered" rewards, which, however, are not treated in the same way as "purchased" goods because, here, the reference point is the emotional capital of the fandom.

This inclusion into the co-creation model, however, carries risks that result from mutual misunderstanding and a lack of clearly defined rules – as demonstrated by the example of Amanda Palmer. In all the above examples, however, we wanted to show how the rhetoric of independence becomes the basis for a "call for action" that implements the mobilizing dimension of utopia. This utopia may relate to the topos of the independent artist (Braff, Palmer), anti-systemness (Troma, Sekielski, The Limousines), or civic engagement (Sekielski). However, it must always include an "action" element placed on the recipient's side, even when it comes down to "merely" locating emotions in a given project or creator.

The crowdfunding of independent creativity has certainly inherited some of the problems we have pointed out when defining independence in music and film of the past. Remembering this, in our understanding, therefore, crowdfunding includes both a financing, promotion and distribution model but also a new model of relationships built using emotional capital. Thanks to these qualities, in some cases – when both artists and audiences want it – crowdfunding creates a new frame for this type of creativity, enabling them to work together in a form of broadly understood co-creation. In this way, it is contributing to a significant transformation of creative industries. Individual projects have a specific value and sometimes translate into profit, but, for those who support the campaign, the value is not in material gratification (with the exception of some users of platforms similar to MegaTotal) but rather in the experience of participating in the process of creating and contributing to independent culture. Artists who want to take advantage of the opportunities offered by crowdfunding must be aware of the importance of this experience. Independence understood in this way cannot be just a rhetorical trick. Although it plays a key role in the promotion and distribution of independent productions, it does not refer to the same niche audience as it did in the past. Thanks to potentials brought about by new media, this independence can be much larger but also more strongly defined, and thus, paradoxically, even more niche. There are also signs that collaboration and co-creation will continue to gain importance, in particular where generational factors are concerned. It is a question of which audience sectors are most interested in advancing this trend and which prefer to maintain a more traditional model. Still, we believe it will play part in the further development of some segments of the creative industries. Therefore, the most important thing, from this perspective, is to discuss the issue of independent authorship anew. It is not only about rights to a text and the financial and legal framework of its production but also about being aware that it is necessary to build a fan base and engage in relational labor (Baym 2018) before the final version of the text is created. Therefore, the greatest challenge for independent artists is understanding the fact that independent production is undergoing transformations that will require them to redefine their role. However, these transformations may lead to the opening of completely new possibilities for independent creativity.

References

Agrawal, Ajay K., Christian Catalini, and Avi Goldfarb. 2015. "Crowdfunding: Geography, Social Networks, and the Timing of Investment Decisions." *Journal of Economics & Management Strategy* 24 (2): 253–274. https://doi.org/10.1111/jems.12093.

Aitamurto, Tanja. 2011. "The Impact Of Crowdfunding On Journalism." *Journalism Practice* 5 (4): 429–445. https://doi.org/10.1080/17512786.2010.551018.

Albini, Steve. 1993. "The Problem with Music." *The Baffler* 5. https://thebaffler.com/salvos/the-problem-with-music.

Allstar Weekend. 2012. "Allstar Weekend Record Label Announcement." https://allstarweekendofficial.tumblr.com/post/15574594080/allstar-weekend-record-label-announcement.

Anderson, Chris. 2006. *The Long Tail: Why the Future of Business Is Selling Less of More*. New York: Hyperion Books.

Baym, Nancy K. 2018. *Playing to the Crowd: Musicians, Audiences, and the Intimate Work of Connection*. New York: New York University Press.

Bell, Nicholas. 2014. "Wish I Was Here | Review." https://www.ioncinema.com/reviews/wish-i-was-here-review.

Bennett, James. 2015. "Introduction: The Utopia of Independent Media: Independence. In Media Independence: Working with Freedom or Working for Free?" In *Media Independence Working with Freedom or Working for Free?* edited by James Bennett and Nicki Strange, 1–28. New York, London: Routledge.

Bennett, Lucy, Bertha Chin, and Bethan Jones. 2015. *Crowdfunding the Future: Media Industries, Ethics and Digital Society*. New York: Peter Lang.

Berkowitz, Joe. 2015. "What You Can Learn From Lil Dicky, The Chart-Topping MC Who Worked At An Ad Agency." *Fast Company*, 10 August 2015. https://www.fastcompany.com/3051615/what-you-can-learn-from-lil-dicky-the-chart-topping-mc-who-worked-at-an-ad-agency.

Berra, John. 2008. *Declarations of Independence: American Cinema and the Partiality of Independent Production*. Bristol: Intellect.

Bordier, Julien. 2008. "Les internautes prennent le pouvoir." *L'Express*, 17 June 2008. https://www.lexpress.fr/culture/musique/les-internautes-prennent-le-pouvoir_512374.html.
Bourdieu, Pierre. 1983. "The Field of Cultural Production, or: The Economic World Reversed." *Poetics* 12 (4): 311–356. https://doi.org/10.1016/0304-422X(83)90012-8.
Bourdieu, Pierre. 1993. *The Field of Cultural Production: Essays on Art and Literature*. New York: Columbia University Press.
Brüntje, Dennis, and Oliver Gajda. 2016. *Crowdfunding in Europe: State of the Art in Theory and Practice*. Cham: Springer International Publishing.
Cammaerts, Bart. 2010. "From Vinyl to One/Zero and Back to Scratch: Independent Belgian Micro Labels in Search of an Ever More Elusive Fan Base." *Media@LSE Electronic Working Paper Series 20*, 1–25. London: London School of Economics and Political Science.
Caves, Richard E. 2000. *Creative Industries. Contracts Between Art and Commerce*. Cambridge, MA and London: Harvard University Press.
Caves, Richard E. 2003. "Contracts Between Art and Commerce." *Journal of Economic Perspectives* 17 (2): 73–84. https://www.jstor.org/stable/3216857.
Church, David. 2010, "Afterword. Memory, Genre and Self-Narrativisation; Or, Why I Should Be a More Content Horror Fan." In *American Horror Film: The Genre at the Turn of the Millennium*, edited by Steffen Hantke, 235–242. Jackson: University Press of Mississippi.
Cova Bernard, and Véronique Cova. 2002, "Tribal Marketing; The Tribalisation of Society and Its Impact on the Conduct of Marketing." *European Journal of Marketing* 36 (5/6): 595–620.
D'Amato, Francesco. 2014. "Investors and Patrons, Gatekeepers and Social Capital: Representations and Experiences of Fans' Participation in Fan Funding." In *The Ashgate Research Companion to Fan Cultures*, edited by Linda Duits, Koos Zwaan, and Stijn Reijnders, 135–148. Surrey: Ashgate.
Dale, Pete. 2008. "It Was Easy, It Was Cheap, So What?: Reconsidering the DIY Principle of Punk and Indie Music." *Popular Music History* 3 (2): 171–193.
Davidson, Roei, and Nathaniel Poor. 2015. "The Barriers Facing Artists' Use of Crowdfunding Platforms: Personality, Emotional Labor, and Going to the Well One Too Many Times." *New Media & Society* 17 (2): 289–307. https://doi.org/10.1177/1461444814558916.
Davidson, Roei, and Nathaniel Poor. 2016. "Factors for Success in Repeat Crowdfunding: Why Sugar Daddies Are Only Good for Bar-Mitzvahs." *Information, Communication & Society* 19 (1): 127–139. https://doi.org/10.1080/1369118X.2015.1093533.
Davidzon, Vladislav. 2013. "Big Jew-Off at Cannes." *Tablet*, 31 May. http://www.tabletmag.com/jewish-arts-and-culture/133355/big-jew-off-at-cannes#undefined.
Dombal, Ryan. 2009. "Amanda Palmer Tells Roadrunner Records: 'Please Drop Me'." *Pitchfork*, 1 April 2009. https://pitchfork.com/news/34979-amanda-palmer-tells-roadrunner-records-please-drop-me/.

References

Dumbreck, Allan, and Gayle McPherson. 2015. *Music Entrepreneurship*. London and New York: Bloomsbury Publishing.

Dunn, Kevin. 2012. "If It Ain't Cheap, It Ain't Punk": Walter Benjamin's Progressive Cultural Production and DIY Punk Record Labels." *Journal of Popular Music Studies* 24 (2): 217–237. https://doi.org/10.1111/j.1533-1598.2012.01326.x.

Fernández Sande, Manuel, and Juan Ignacio Gallego Pérez. 2015. "Crowdfunding as a Source of Financing for Radio and Audio Content in Spain." *Quaderns Del CAC* 18 (41): 43–51.

Fishbein, Rebecca. 2013. "'Veronica Mars' Kickstarter Closes Today, Smashes Crowdfunding Records." *LAist*. http://laist.com/2013/04/12/veronica_mars_kickstarter_closes_to.php.

Fonarow, Wendy. 2006. *Empire of Dirt: The Aesthetics and Rituals of British Indie Music*. Middletown: Wesleyan University Press.

Fox, Mark. 2004. "E-Commerce Business Models for the Music Industry." *Popular Music and Society* 27 (2): 201. https://doi.org/10.1080/03007760410001685831.

Fuchs, Christian. 2010. "Alternative Media as Critical Media." *European Journal of Social Theory* 13 (2): 173–192.

Gaiman, Neil. 2002. *Neil Gaiman's Journal (blog)*. http://journal.neilgaiman.com/2002/04/in-relation-to-current-burning-topic.asp.

Galuszka, Patryk. 2015. "Music Aggregators and Intermediation of the Digital Music Market." *International Journal of Communication* 9: 254–273.

Galuszka, Patryk. 2020. "'Music as the Binder.' A Conversation with Macio Moretti." In *Made in Poland. Studies in Popular Music*, edited by Patryk Galuszka, 213–223. London and New York: Routledge.

Galuszka, Patryk, and Blanka Brzozowska. 2016. "Early Career Artists and the Exchange of Gifts on a Crowdfunding Platform." *Continuum: Journal of Media and Cultural Studies* 30 (6): 744–753.

Galuszka, Patryk, and Blanka Brzozowska. 2017a. "Crowdfunding and the Democratization of the Music Market." *Media, Culture & Society* 39 (6): 833–849. https://doi.org/10.1177/0163443716674364.

Galuszka, Patryk, and Blanka Brzozowska. 2017b. "Crowdfunding: Towards a Redefinition of the Artist's Role–the Case of MegaTotal." *International Journal of Cultural Studies* 20 (1): 83–99.

Galuszka, Patryk, and Victor Bystrov. 2014a. "Crowdfunding: A Case Study of a New Model of Financing Music Production." *Journal of Internet Commerce* 13 (3–4): 233–252. https://doi.org/10.1080/15332861.2014.961349.

Galuszka, Patryk, and Victor Bystrov. 2014b. "The Rise of Fanvestors: A Study of a Crowdfunding Community." *First Monday* 19 (5).

Gerber, Elizabeth M., and Julie Hui. 2013. "Crowdfunding: Motivations and Deterrents for Participation." *ACM Trans. Comput.-Hum. Interact* 20 (6): 34:1–34:32. https://doi.org/10.1145/2530540.

Gerber Liz, and Julie Hui. 2016. "Crowdfunding: How and Why People Participate." In *International Perspectives on Crowdfunding,* edited by Jérôme

Méric, Isabelle Maque, and Julienne Brabet, 37–64. Bingley, UK: Emerald Group Publishing Limited.

Giannetti, Louis. 1999. *Understanding Movies (8th edition)*. Upper Saddle River, NJ: Prentice Hall.

Gillespie, Tarleton. 2010. "The Politics of 'Platforms.'" *New Media & Society* 12 (3): 347–364. https://doi.org/10.1177/1461444809342738.

Gillespie, Tarleton. 2018. *Custodians of the Internet: Platforms, Content Moderation, and the Hidden Decisions That Shape Social Media*. New Haven and London: Yale University Press.

Goldstein, Gregg, and Chris Morris. 2013. "Zach Braff Kickstarter Success: Will Crowdfunding Transform Showbiz?" *Variety*, 5 June. http://variety.com/2013/biz/news/zach-braff-kickstarter-success-will-crowdfunding-transform-showbiz-1200492256.

Gómez-Diago, Gloria. 2015. "Communication in Crowdfunding Online Platforms." In *Creativity in the Digital Age*, edited by Nelson Zagalo and Pedro Branco, 171–190. Springer Series on Cultural Computing. London: Springer. https://doi.org/10.1007/978-1-4471-6681-8_10.

Gosling, Tim. 2004. "'Not For Sale': The Underground Network of Anarcho-Punk." In *Music Scenes: Local, Translocal and Virtual*, edited by Andy Bennett, and Richard A. Peterson, 168–183. Nashville, TN: Vanderbilt University Press.

Hagedorn, Anja, and Andreas Pinkwart. 2016. "The Financing Process of Equity-Based Crowdfunding: An Empirical Analysis." In *Crowdfunding in Europe: State of the Art in Theory and Practice*, edited by Dennis Brüntje, and Oliver Gajda, 71–85. Cham: Springer International Publishing. https://doi.org/10.1007/978-3-319-18017-5_5.

Haynes, Jo, and Lee Marshall. 2018. "Reluctant Entrepreneurs: Musicians and Entrepreneurship in the 'New' Music Industry." *The British Journal of Sociology* 69: 459–482. https://doi.org/10.1111/1468-4446.12286.

Hesmondhalgh, David. 1997. "Post-Punk's Attempt to Democratise the Music Industry: The Success and Failure of Rough Trade." *Popular Music* 16 (3): 255–274. https://doi.org/10.1017/S0261143000008400.

Hesmondhalgh, David. 1999. "Indie: The institutional Politics and Aesthetics of a Popular Music Genre." *Cultural Studies* 13 (1): 34–61.

Hesmondhalgh, David. 2013. *Why Music Matters*. Malden, MA: Wiley-Blackwell.

Hesmondhalgh, David. 2019. *The Cultural Industries*. London: SAGE.

Hesmondhalgh, David, and Leslie M. Meier. 2015. "Popular Music, Independence and the Concept of the Alternative in Contemporary Capitalism." In *Independence: Working with Freedom or Working for Free?* edited by James Bennett and Niki Strange, 94–112. London and New York: Routledge.

Hilburn, Roxanne. 2011. "Interview with Giovanni Giusti of The Limousines at Outside Lands." *Grimy Goods*. https://www.grimygoods.com/2011/08/23/interview-with-giovanni-giusti-of-the-limousines-at-outside-lands/.

References 107

Hills, Matt. 2015. "Veronica Mars, Fandom, and the 'Affective Economics' of Crowdfunding Poachers." *New Media & Society* 17 (2): 183–197. https://doi.org/10.1177/1461444814558909.

Hracs, Brian J., Doreen Jakob, and Atle Hauge. 2013. "Standing Out in the Crowd: The Rise of Exclusivity-Based Strategies to Compete in the Contemporary Marketplace for Music and Fashion." *Environment and Planning A* 45 (5): 1144–1161.

Hunter, Andrea. 2016. "'It's Like Having a Second Full-Time Job.'" *Journalism Practice* 10 (2): 217–232. https://doi.org/10.1080/17512786.2015.1123107.

Hurst, Samantha. 2016. "Amanda Palmer: 'My Kickstarter Was Terribly Budgeted'." https://www.crowdfundinsider.com/2016/02/81782-amanda-palmer-my-kickstarter-was-terribly-budgeted/.

IMDB. 2014. "Zach Braff's Kickstarter-funded Wish I Was Here is a Strange, Confused, and More Than Occasionally Profound and Moving Film about Family, Life, Relationships and Death." IMDB, 20 July 2014. https://www.imdb.com/review/rw3053469/?ref_=rw_urv.

Jacob Matthews, Stéphane Costantini, and Alix Bénistant 2019. "Globalization and the Logics of Capitalism" In *Cultural Crowdfunding: Platform Capitalism, Labour and Globalization*, edited by Vincent Rouzé, 79–98. London: University of Westminster Press.

Jenkins, Henry. 2006. *Convergence Culture: Where Old and New Media Collide*. New York: New York University Press.

Jenkins, Henry, Sam Ford, and Joshua Green. 2013. *Spreadable Media: Creating Value and Meaning in a Networked Culture*. New York: New York University Press.

Jian, Lian, and Jieun Shin. 2015. "Motivations Behind Donors' Contributions to Crowdfunded Journalism." *Mass Communication and Society* 18 (2): 165–185. https://doi.org/10.1080/15205436.2014.911328.

Johnston, Garth. 2013. "The Veronica Mars Movie Is Real And Needs Your Help!." *Gothamist*, 13 March. http://gothamist.com/2013/03/13/holy_crap_the_veronica_mars_movie_i.php.

Karppinen, Kari, and Hallvard Moe. 2016. "What We Talk About When Talk About 'Media Independence'." *Javnost – The Public* 23 (2): 105–119, DOI:10.1080/13183222.2016.1162986.

Kickstarter. 2011. "The Scurvies to Release New Album this Summer! Check it Out!" https://www.kickstarter.com/projects/529550978/the-scurvies-to-release-new-album-this-summer-chec/description.

Kickstarter. 2012a. "All You Ever Wanted to Know About All This Kickstarter Money & Where it's Going." https://www.kickstarter.com/projects/amandapalmer/amanda-palmer-the-new-record-art-book-and-tour/posts/232020.

Kickstarter. 2012b. "TROMA Entertainment Return to Nuke 'Em High DUCKSTARTER!" https://www.kickstarter.com/projects/852899646/troma-entertainment-return-to-nuke-em-high-ducksta/description.

Kickstarter. 2013a. "ALLSTAR WEEKEND'S NEW CD! AUTOGRAPHED COPY ONLY $20!" Last modified 24 October 2013. https://www.kickstarter.com/projects/allstarweekend/allstar-weekends-new-album-ballin/description.

Kickstarter. 2013b. "MY TAKE ON THE RECENT NEWS & HOW IT EFFECTS YOUR KICKSTARTER PLEDGE." 1 February 2013. https://www.kickstarter.com/projects/allstarweekend/allstar-weekends-new-album-ballin/posts/397139.

Kickstarter. 2014a. "Wish I Was Here" (comments section). 29 September. https://www.kickstarter.com/projects/1869987317/wish-i-was-here-1/comments?comment=Q29tbWVudC04NzYxNzQw

Kickstarter. 2014b. "Wish I Was Here" (comments section). 15 January. https://www.kickstarter.com/projects/1869987317/wish-i-was-here-1/comments?comment=Q29tbWVudC04NzYxNzQw.

Kickstarter. 2015a. "Kickstarter is Now a Benefit Corporation." *The Kickstarter Blog*. https://www.kickstarter.com/blog/kickstarter-is-now-a-benefit-corporation?ref=charter.

Kickstarter. 2015b. "Lil Dicky's Kickstarter – Album, Videos, Touring." Last modified 6 August 2015. https://www.kickstarter.com/projects/232550405/lil-dickys-kickstarter-album-videos-touring/description.

Kickstarter. 2015c. "The Limousines - Hush - The New Album." Last modified 3 July 2015. https://www.kickstarter.com/projects/ericvictorino/the-limousines-hush-the-new-album/description.

Kickstarter. 2015d. "Wish I Was Here" (comments section). 15 January. https://www.kickstarter.com/projects/1869987317/wish-i-was-here-1/comments?comment=Q29tbWVudC04NzYxNzQw.

Kickstarter. 2015e. "'Return to Nuke 'Em High: Volume 2' by Troma Entertainment." https://www.kickstarter.com/projects/return2nukeemhigh2/return-to-nuke-em-high-volume-2-by-troma-entertain/description.

Kickstarter. 2015f. (comment section). https://www.kickstarter.com/projects/return2nukeemhigh2/return-to-nuke-em-high-volume-2-by-troma-entertain/comments.

Kickstarter. 2018. "Theatre Is Evil: The Album, Art Book and Tour." Last modified 12 December 2018. https://www.kickstarter.com/projects/amandapalmer/amanda-palmer-the-new-record-art-book-and-tour?ref=discovery&term=amanda%20palmer.

King, Ashley. 2019. "The Rise and Fall of PledgeMusic—How the Future of Music Crowdfunding Turned Into a Nightmare." *Digital Music News*, 25 October 2019. https://www.digitalmusicnews.com/2019/10/25/rise-and-fall-of-pledgemusic/.

King, Geoff. 2005. *American Independent Cinema*. Bloomington and Indianapolis: Indiana University Press.

King, Geoff. 2015. "Differences of Kind and Degree: Articulations of Independence in American Cinema." In *Media Independence. Working with Freedom or Working for Free?* edited by James Bennett and Nicki Strange, 52–70. New York, London: Routledge.

References

Kohler, Thomas. 2015. "Crowdsourcing-Based Business Models: How To Create And Capture Value." *California Management Review* 57 (4): 63–84.

Konferencja Episkopatu Polski. 2019. "Biskupi do wiernych: nie uczyniliśmy wszystkiego, aby zapobiec krzywdom." 26 May. https://episkopat.pl/biskupi-do-wiernych-nie-uczynilismy-wszystkiego-aby-zapobiec-krzywdom/.

Kotler, Philip, Hermawan Kartajaya, and Iwan Setiawan. 2016. *Marketing 4.0 Moving from Traditional to Digital*. Hoboken, NJ: Willey & Sons.

Kreiss, Daniel. 2015. "A Vision of and for the Networked World: John Perry Barlow's A Declaration of the Independence of Cyberspace at Twenty." In *Media Independence. Working with Freedom or Working for Free?* edited by James Bennett and Nicki Strange, 117–135. London and New York: Routledge.

Kurdupski, Michał. 2019. "170 tys. widzów premiery 'Tylko nie mów nikomu' w Telewizji WP." https://www.wirtualnemedia.pl/artykul/tylko-nie-mow-nikomu-ilu-widzow-ogladalo-debiut-filmu.

Landström, Hans, Annaleena Parhankangas, and Colin Mason. 2019. *Handbook of Research on Crowdfunding*. Cheltenham, UK and Northampton, MA: Edward Elgar Publishing.

Lee, Stephen. 1995. "Re-Examining the Concept of the 'Independent' Record Company: The Case of Wax Trax! Records." *Popular Music* 14 (1): 13–31.

Leibovitz, Talia, Antoni Roig Telo, and Jordi Sánchez-Navarro. 2015. "Up Close and Personal: Exploring the Bonds Between Promoters and Backers in Audiovisual Crowdfunded Projects." In *Crowdfunding the Future: Media Industries, Ethics and Digital Society*, edited by Lucy Bennett, Bertha Chin, and Bethan Jones, 15–30. New York: Peter Lang.

Levy, Emanuel. 1999. *Cinema of Outsiders, The Rise of American Independent Film*. New York: New York University Press.

Lucca, Valeria de. 2011. "L'Alcasta and the Emergence of Collective Patronage in Mid-Seventeenth-Century Rome." *The Journal of Musicology* 28 (2): 195–230. https://doi.org/10.1525/jm.2011.28.2.195.

Lunney, Glynn S. 2014. "Copyright on the Internet: Consumer Copying and Collectives." In *The Evolution and Equilibrium of Copyright in the Digital Age*, edited by Susy Frankel and Daniel Gervais, 285–311. Cambridge, UK: Cambridge University Press.

Marelli, Alessandro, and Andrea Ordanini. 2016. "What Makes Crowdfunding Projects Successful 'Before' and 'During' the Campaign?" In *Crowdfunding in Europe: State of the Art in Theory and Practice*, edited by Dennis Brüntje, and Oliver Gajda, 175–192. Cham: Springer International Publishing. https://doi.org/10.1007/978-3-319-18017-5_12.

Market Research Inc. 2019. *Crowdfunding Market – Europe Insights, Growth, Size, Comparative Analysis, Trends and Forecast, 2019-2027*. San Francisco, CA: Market Research Inc.

Marshall, Lee. 2005. *Bootlegging: Romanticism and Copyright in the Music Industry*. London: SAGE.

Massolution. 2015. *2015CF the Crowdfunding Industry Report*. Los Angeles, CA: Massolution.

McAfee, R. Preston, Hugo M. Mialon, and Michael A. Williams. 2004. "What Is a Barrier to Entry?" *The American Economic Review* 94 (2): 461–465.

McNelly, Lucas. 2013. Sundance Report: The Crowd Consensus. http://turnstylenews.com/2013/01/24/sundance-report-the-crowd-consensus/.

Meier, Leslie M. 2017. *Popular Music as Promotion: Music and Branding in the Digital Age*. Malden, MA and Oxford, UK: John Wiley & Sons.

Méric, Jérôme, Isabelle Maque, and Julienne Brabet. 2016. *International Perspectives on Crowdfunding*. Bingley, UK: Emerald Group Publishing Limited.

Moore, Allan. 2002. "Authenticity as Authentication." *Popular Music* 21 (2): 209–223. https://doi.org/10.1017/S0261143002002131.

Moore, Ryan. 2007. "Friends Don't Let Friends Listen to Corporate Rock." *Journal of Contemporary Ethnography* 36 (4): 438–474. https://doi.org/10.1177/0891241607303520.

Morris, Jeremy Wade. 2013. "Artists as Entrepreneurs, Fans as Workers." *Popular Music and Society* 37 (3): 273–290. https://doi.org/10.1080/03007766.2013.778534.

Navar-Gill, Annemarie. 2018. "Fandom as Symbolic Patronage: Expanding Understanding of Fan Relationships with Industry through the Veronica Mars Kickstarter Campaign." *Popular Communication* 16 (3): 211–224. https://doi.org/10.1080/15405702.2018.1453069.

Nedmic, Michel. 2012. "My Major Company: un point sur les mises." *Alloprod*, 3 May 2012. https://www.alloprod.com/my-major-company-un-point-sur-les-mises/.

Negus, Keith. 1999. *Music Genres and Corporate Cultures*. London and New York: Routledge.

Newman, Brian. 2012. "Posts I Like: 'Disrupted: Indie Filmmakers.'" *Truly Free Film* (blog). http://networkedblogs.com/yeA6l.

New Release Today. 2011. "Artist Profile. The Scurvies." https://www.newreleasetoday.com/artistdetail.php?artist_id=3379#:~:text=The%20Scurvies%20are%20a%20old,of%20Boot%20To%20Head%20Records.

O'Malley, Sheila. 2014. "Wish I Was Here (Review)." *RogerEbert.com (blog)*. https://www.rogerebert.com/reviews/wish-i-was-here-2014.

O'Malley Greenburg, Zack. 2015. "Amanda Palmer Uncut: The Kickstarter Queen On Spotify, Patreon And Taylor Swift." *Forbes*, 16 April 2015. https://www.forbes.com/sites/zackomalleygreenburg/2015/04/16/amanda-palmer-uncut-the-kickstarter-queen-on-spotify-patreon-and-taylor-swift/.

Ordanini, Andrea, Lucia Miceli, Marta Pizzetti, and A. Parasuraman. 2011. "Crowd-Funding: Transforming Customers into Investors through Innovative Service Platforms." *Journal of Service Management* 22 (4): 443–470. https://doi.org/10.1108/09564231111155079.

Osterwalder, Alexander, Yves Pigneur, and Christopher L. Tucci. 2005. "Clarifying Business Models: Origins, Present, and Future of the Concept." *Communication of the Association for Information Systems* 15: 1–40. https://doi.org/10.17705/1CAIS.01601.

Pallus, Patryk. 2019. "Film Tomasza Sekielskiego o pedofilii w Kościele 'Tylko nie mów nikomu' z rekordem oglądalności." https://www.onet.pl/?utm_source=pl.wikipedia.org_viasg_businessinsider&utm_medium=referal&utm_campaign=leo_automatic&srcc=ucs&pid=1571ae78-19ca-424b-bc8c-0440b5e207af&sid=ca05277f-7c3f-495c-9acc-986177acd173&utm_v=2.
Palmer, Amanda. 2015. "No, I Am Not Crowdfunding This Baby (An Open Letter to a Worried Fan)." https://medium.com/we-are-the-media/no-i-am-not-crowdfunding-this-baby-an-open-letter-to-a-worried-fan-9ca75cb0f938.
Papadopoulos, Theo. 2004. "Are Music Recording Contracts Equitable? An Economic Analysis of the Practice of Recoupment." *MEIEA Journal* 4 (1): 83–105.
Passman, Donald S. 2019. *All You Need To Know About The Music Business. 10th Edition.* New York: Simon & Schuster.
Patreon. 2020. "Eric Victorino is creating Art & Music. About." https://www.patreon.com/ericvictorino.
Patronite. 2018. "Sekielski Brothers Studio." https://patronite.pl/sekielski/description.
Patronite. 2019. "Podziekowanie." https://patronite.pl/post/7524/podziekowanie.
Peirson-Hagger, Ellen. 2020. "'I Lost My Identity': The Artists Who Left Major Record Deals to Form Their Own Indie Labels." *New Statesman*, 8 July 2020. https://www.newstatesman.com/culture/music-theatre/2020/07/i-lost-my-identity-artists-who-left-major-record-deals-form-their-own.
Perren, Alisa. 2012. *Indie, Inc. Miramax and the Transformation of Hollywood in the 1990s.* Austin: University of Texas Press.
Pierson, John. 1997. *Spike, Mike, Slackers, & Dykes.* New York: Gardners Books.
Pitrus, Andrzej, 2010. *Porzucone znaczenia. Autorzy amerykańskiego kina niezależnego przełomu wieków.* Krakow: Rabid.
Poell, Thomas, and José van Dijck. 2015. "Social Media and Journalistic Independence." In *Media Independence. Working with Freedom or Working for Free?* edited by James Bennett and Nicki Strange, 182–201. New York, London: Routledge.
Popiel, Kat. "The gogofactor & How to Get Featured on Our Homepage." *Indiegogo (blog).* https://blog.indiegogo.com/2011/08/the-magic-gogofactor.html.
Prey, Robert. 2020. "Locating Power in Platformization: Music Streaming Playlists and Curatorial Power." *Social Media + Society* 6 (2): 2056305120933291. https://doi.org/10.1177/2056305120933291.
Read, Andrew. 2020. "ArtistShare: Brian Camelio Speaks…" *Jazz in Europe*, 28 April 2020. https://jazzineurope.mfmmedia.nl/2020/04/artistshare-brian-camelio-speaks/.
Ronson, Jon. 2013. "Amanda Palmer: Visionary or Egotist?" *The Guardian*, 22 June 2013. https://www.theguardian.com/music/2013/jun/22/amanda-palmer-visionary-egotist-interview.
Rothman, Lily. 2013. "The Toxic Investor: A Legendary Indie-Film Company Turns to Crowdfunding." *Time,* 27 February. http://entertainment.time.

com/2013/02/27/the-toxic-investor-a-legendary-indie-film-company-turns-to-crowdfunding/.
Rouzé, Vincent. 2019. "Far from an Alternative: Intermediation Apparatuses." In *Cultural Crowdfunding: Platform Capitalism, Labour and Globalization*, edited by Vincent Rouzé, 35–58. London: University of Westminster Press.
Scott, Suzanne. 2015. "The Moral Economy of Crowdfunding and the Transformative Capacity of Fan-Ancing." *New Media & Society* 17 (2): 167–182. https://doi.org/10.1177/1461444814558908.
SellaBand. 2009. "How it Works." https://web.archive.org/web/20090226044851/http://www.sellaband.com/site/how-it-works.html.
SellaBand. 2015. "About Us." https://web.archive.org/web/20150907082349/https://www.sellaband.com/en/pages/about_us.
Simon, Phil. 2013. "My Interview With Mark Kelly of Marillion." https://www.philsimon.com/blog/trends/my-interview-with-mark-kelly-of-marillion/.
Smith, Anthony N. 2015. "The Backer–Developer Connection: Exploring Crowdfunding's Influence on Video Game Production." *New Media & Society* 17 (2): 198–214. https://doi.org/10.1177/1461444814558910.
Suhr, Hiesun Cecilia. 2012. "Understanding the Hegemonic Struggle between Mainstream Vs. Independent Forces: The Music Industry and Musicians in the Age of Social Media." *The International Journal of Technology, Knowledge and Society* 7 (6): 123–136.
Taylor, Ryan. 2015. "Equity-based Crowdfunding: Potential Implications for Small Business Capital." *Advocacy: the Voice of Small Business in Government* 5: 1–8.
Terranova, Tiziana. 2000. "Free Labor: Producing Culture for the Digital Economy." *Social Text* 18 (2): 33–58.
Thorley, Mark. 2012. "An Audience in the Studio – the Effect of the Artistshare Fan-Funding Platform on Creation, Performance, Recording and Production." *Journal on the Art of Record Production* 7. https://www.arpjournal.com/asarpwp/an-audience-in-the-studio-%E2%80%93-the-effect-of-the-artistshare-fan-funding-platform-on-creation-performance-recording-and-production/.
Thürridl, Carina, and Bernadette Kamleitner. 2016. "What Goes Around Comes Around? Rewards as Strategic Assets in Crowdfunding." *California Management Review* 94 (2): 88–110. https://doi.org/10.1525/cmr.2016.58.2.88.
Trampe, Michael. 2014. "Lil Dicky Talks Upgrading His Rap Career Via $100,000 Kickstarter Campaign." *HipHopdx*, 10 April 2014. https://hiphopdx.com/interviews/id.2348/title.lil-dicky-talks-upgrading-his-rap-career-via-100000-kickstarter-campaign#.
Tuomola, Arto. 2004. "Disintermediation and Reintermediation of the Sound Recording Value Chain: Two Case Studies." *Journal of Media Business Studies* 1 (1): 27–46. DOI: 10.1080/16522354.2004.11073419.
Tzioumakis, Yannis. 2006. *American Independent Cinema*. New Brunswick: Rutgers University Press.
Vargo, Stephen L., and Robert F. Lusch. 2004. "Evolving to a New Dominant Logic for Marketing." *Journal of Marketing* 68 (1): 1–17.

Vargo, Stephen L., and Robert F. Lusch. 2008. "Service-dominant Logic: Continuing the Evolution." *Journal of the Academy of Marketing Science* 36 (1): 1–10.

Veenstra, Gerry. 2015. "Class Position and Musical Tastes: A Sing-Off between the Cultural Omnivorism and Bourdieusian Homology Frameworks." *Canadian Review of Sociology/Revue Canadienne de Sociologie* 52 (2): 134–159. https://doi.org/10.1111/cars.12068.

Voynar, Kim. 2012. "Digital Distribution Revolution." *Movie City News*, 31 May. http://archive.moviecitynews.com/category/mcn-blogs/film-essent/2012/05/.

Wang, Cynthia. 2016. "The Promise of Kickstarter: Extents to Which Social Networks Enable Alternate Avenues of Economic Viability for Independent Musicians Through Crowdfunding."*Social Media + Society*, 2 (3), 1–12 September. https://doi.org/10.1177/2056305116662394.

Williams, Justin A., and Ross Wilson. 2016. "Music and Crowdfunded Websites. Digital Patronage and Artist-Fan Interactivity." In *The Oxford Handbook of Music and Virtuality,* edited by Sheila Whiteley, and Shara Rambarran, 593–612. New York: Oxford University Press.

YouTube. 2019. "TYLKO NIE MÓW NIKOMU | dokument Tomasza Sekielskiego | cały film | 2019." https://www.youtube.com/watch?v=BrUvQ3W3nV4.

Zara, Christopher. 2013. "Zach Braff Kickstarter Campaign: Twitter Backlash As 'Wish I Was Here' Tests Limits Of Crowd Funding." *International Business Times.* http://www.ibtimes.com/zach-braff-kickstarter-campaign-twitter-backlash-wish-i-was-here-tests-limits-crowd-funding-1215021.

Zvilichovsky, David, Shai Danziger, and Yael Steinhart. 2018. "Making-the-Product-Happen: A Driver of Crowdfunding Participation." *Journal of Interactive Marketing* 41 (February): 81–93. https://doi.org/10.1016/j.intmar.2017.10.002.

Index

African-American audiences, 32
African-American roots of music, 66
algorithms, 45
Allstar Weekend, 87–89, 93
altruistic motives, 12
American Beauty, 31
American emo pop band, 87
American independent cinema, 23–24
anti-clerical views, 59
anti-commercialism, 65, 83, 91
Ark Productions, 45
art for art's sake logic, 65
art houses, 24, 60
ArtistShare, 5–6, 78–82
atheistic views, 59
auteur style, 24, 28
Avengers, 32

baby boomers, 30–31
backers, 7–8, 10–11, 13, 50, 52–53, 84, 87, 91
Baumbach, Noah, 27
bankruptcy, 6, 68, 72
belonging, sense of, 12
Bennett, James, 20–21, 36, 57
Berra, John, 18, 23–24, 26, 29, 34–38, 42–43, 47–48
Bieber, Justin, 47, 92
Big Bang Theory, 47
Black audiences, 32
Black Panther, 32
Black roots of music, 66
Blair Witch Project, 36, 42
books, MyMajorCompany, 80
boundaries, blurring of, 37
Bourdieu, Pierre, 65

Braff, Zach, 29, 40, 45–51, 53, 96, 100–101
Business Record, industry magazine, 63

Cannes, 52
Carolco Pictures, 34
Cassavetes, John, 28, 34, 46
Church hierarchies, 55, 59
cinema
   independent, 18–61
   Braff, Zach, 45–51
   crowdfunded, 40–61
   definition of independence, 19–26
   distribution, 33–36
   history, 26–28
   independent filmmaker, 28
   MeToo movement, 32
   Sekielski brothers, 55–61
   topics in independent cinema, 31–33
   Troma, 51–55
Clerks, 25–26, 30
Coen brothers, 26
Collect Rewards, 12
collection, period for, 14
collective patronage, 4–6
Comic Con, 48
comics, MyMajorCompany, 80
commercialism, 21, 25, 27, 30, 59, 64, 83
community feedback, gaining, 11
community of recipients, 55, 69, 98
connections with backers, 10

Index

contributor motivations, 90
contributors, 6–8, 10–15, 50, 72–77, 79–81, 87, 94, 97, 100
  special offers to attract, 14
copyright, 50, 76
cost barriers, 15
Coulton, Jonathan, 3
counter cultural heyday, rock and soul, 66
Creation Records, 68
Creative Commons, 3
creativity, 1–2, 6–17, 19, 22, 25, 52, 56, 96, 98, 100–102
crowdfunding platforms, 4, 6–8, 10, 72–73, 83, 100
crowdinvesting, 9
crypto-independents, 63
cult classics, 52
cult interest, 14–15, 27, 29, 31–32, 36, 45, 47–48, 50, 52–53, 55, 57, 60, 62, 64, 66, 68, 71, 83, 94–95
cultural markets, entry to, 15–17

Dangerfield Records, 89
dark humor, 48
DC Comics, 32
Dead Man Walking, 32, 47
definition of independence, 19–26
democratization, dilemma of, 17
Deren, Maya, 28
digitization, 99
dilemma of democratization, 17
Dischord, 68
Disney Music Group, 88
do-it-yourself ethos, 57–58, 67–68, 83
document artistic achievements, 69
documentaries, 52, 55, 57, 61, 100
Domino Records, 68
donation-based crowdfunding, 5, 8, 12, 15, 83, 87
Double Feature Films, 46
Duplass brothers, 27

early crowdfunding, 5
Easy Rider, 26
elements of authenticity, 65–66
email, 6, 85
equity-based crowdfunding, 9
Eraserhead, 26

Facebook, 7, 15, 53, 60
fairer fund distribution rules, 69, 81
Faison, Donald, 47
fan culture, 48, 55
fanbase, 41, 53, 89
feedback, community, gaining, 11
Fight Club, 31
filmmakers, independent, 28
financing, 5–17
  contributors, 11–14
  cultural markets,
    entry to, 15–17
  participating entities, 7
  platforms, 7–10
  project initiators, 10–11
  success factors, 14–15
  typology of crowdfunding, 7
Fincher, David, 29, 31
Focus Films, 46
forming connections with backers, 10
Foucault, Michael, 38
Fox Searchlight Pictures, 45
Franz Ferdinand Band, 68
French New Wave, 27
Fuchs, Christian, 57–58

Galuszka, Patryk, 12, 46, 58, 71, 73, 78, 87, 94
Game of Thrones, 48
Garden State, 45, 47–48
Generation X, 30–31, 48, 61
  distinguishing features, 29
generational director, 40, 47
genre of horror, 40
Get Sharp, 89
Giusti, Giovanni, 89
gogofactor, 44
Good Will Hunting, 61
government representatives, 59

Happiness, 32
Hollywood culture, 26–27, 32, 38, 48, 52–53, 88–89
Hopper, Dennis, 26
Horror Film Challenge, 54
horror genre, 40
Hudson, Kate, 47

116   Index

independence, 1–4, 10, 18–27, 34, 36–41, 46–47, 52, 55, 57–98, 100–101
  rhetoric of, 44, 96
independent cinema, 18–61
  author style, 28
  Braff, Zach, 45–51
  crowdfunded, 40–61
  definition of independence, 19–26
  distribution, 33–36
  history, 26–28
  independent filmmaker, 28
  MeToo movement, 32
  promotion, 33–36
  Sekielski brothers, 55–61
  Troma, 51–55
independent music, 62–95
  independent musicians, 83–94
    independence issues, 87–94
    problem of accountability, 83–87
    labels, 72–82 (*See also under* individual label name)
    ArtistShare, 5–6, 78–82
    MegaTotal, 73–78
    MyMajorCompany, 78–82
    SellaBand, 78–82
  theorizing independence, 62–72
    economic criteria, 62–64
    type of independence, 68–72
    value of independence, 64–68
IndieGoGo, 6, 44, 52, 72, 78
indies, 27, 32
Indiewood, creation of, 33
individual expression, 65
informal contracts, 69
initiators, 2, 6–7, 10, 12, 14–15, 74, 77, 79, 87
instinctiveness/non-rational nature of music, 65

Jackson, Samuel L. 32
Jarmusch, Jim, 26
journalistic projects, 12
judicial intervention, 50

Kaufman, Lloyd, 52–54, 100

Kelly, Mark, 6
Kickstarter Indiegogo, 72
Kickstarter platform, 1, 6–7, 10, 42, 44–45, 49–50, 52–53, 55–56, 72, 77–78, 84–85, 87–93, 95
King, Geoff, 6, 18, 22, 26, 28, 30–34, 36–38, 42, 89
Kiva, 6
Kreiss, Daniel, 20

labels, 72–82. *See also under* individual label name
  ArtistShare, 5–6, 78–82
  MegaTotal, 73–78
  MyMajorCompany, 78–82
  SellaBand, 78–82
Latour, Bruno, 45
learning new fundraising skills, 10
Lee, Spike, 29, 32, 39, 72
legal issues, 50
legal provisions, 15
lending-based crowdfunding, 9
Levy, Emanuel, 18, 25–27, 31–32, 61
LGBT themes, 32
Lil Dicky, 91, 100
Limousines, 90, 101
Linklater, Richard, 27, 29
Lord of the Rings, 31, 52
Lynch, David, 26

mailing lists, use of, 6
Marillion band, 6
marketing conditions, 15
marketing tricks, 51
mass culture, 27
McGee, Alan, 68
MegaTotal platform, 12, 73–78, 80–81, 86, 95
Mekas, John, 28
MeToo movement, 32
Miramax, 27, 30
mobilization, 69motivations, 10–13, 87, 91, 99
mumblecore subgenre, development of, 27
music
  independent, 62–95
    labels, 72–82 (*See also under* individual labels)

Index 117

ArtistShare, 5–6, 78–82
MegaTotal, 73–78
MyMajorCompany, 78–82
SellaBand, 78–82
musicians, 83–94
 independence issues, 87–94
 problem of accountability, 83–87
 theorizing independence, 62–72
 economic criteria, 62–64
 type of independence, 68–72
 value of independence, 64–68
musicians, independent, 83–94
 independence issues, 87–94
 problem of accountability, 83–87
MyMajorCompany, 78–82
Myrick, Daniel, 35

NBC Universal, 46
need for mobilization and participation, 69
News Corporation media group, 45
niche audience, 42, 44, 46, 48, 51–52, 61
noncorporate ethos, 69

Occupy Cannes!, 52
O'Malley Greenburg, Zack, 46, 84
originality, 19, 65

Palahniuk, Chuck, 31
Palmer, Amanda, 1–2, 16, 84–85, 87, 96–97, 100–101
Parsons, Jim, 47
participation, 7, 57–58, 69, 98
patronage crowdfunding, 10
Patronite platform, 40, 55
Permanent Council of Polish Episcopal Conference, 59
Perren, Alisa, 27
Pink Flamingos, 26
place of crowdfunding, 2
platforms, 2, 4, 6–10, 13–14, 45, 55, 72–73, 81, 83, 99–100. *See also under* individual platform name
Poland, 55, 73
Polish Catholic Church, 55
Polish documentary, 55, 100

Polish YouTube viewership, 58
popular and mass culture, 27
popular culture, 7, 10, 21, 24, 27, 56, 59–60, 66, 74, 88–89, 94
portal Patronite, 55
pre-capitalist patrons, 65
pre-ordering, 12
project initiators, 6–7, 10–12, 15, 77, 79, 87
proto-crowdfunding, 5
Pulitzer, Joseph, 5
Pulp Fiction, 26

radio broadcasts, 5
Reservoir Dogs, 26
Return to Nuke 'Em High, 52
Return to Nuke 'Em High: Volume 2, 53
reward-based crowdfunding, 8
Reznor, Trent, 3
rhetoric, of independence, 44
rhetorical independence, 20, 36, 87
rivalry for consumers, 17
Robbins, Tim, 32
Romanticism, 65
Rotten Tomatoes, 49
royalty-based crowdfunding, 9

Sanchez, Eduardo, 35
School of Rock, 29
Scrubs, 47
Scurvies, 92–93
Sekielski brothers, 40, 55–61, 100–101
self-management, 69
self-reported motivations, 12
SellaBand platform, 6, 78–82, 95
sense of belonging, 12
service dominant logic, paradigm of, 43
sex, lies, and videotape, 26
Shaft, 32
Slacker, 29
slogans, thresholds marked with, 56
Small Wonder, 68
Smith, Kevin, 11, 26, 29, 100
social media, 1–2, 15, 19, 32, 38, 44–45, 53–54, 68, 91, 93, 96, 98, 100
socio-cultural motivations, 12

sociopolitical independence, 19–20
Soderbergh, Steven, 26, 45
Solondz, Todd, 32
special offers, to attract contributors, 14
Spotify, 7
Spot.Us, 12
Star Trek, 48
Star Wars, 30, 48, 52
Statue of Liberty, 5
Story, Tom, 32, 48, 89–90
success factors, 14–15
Sundance Festival, 27, 34

Tarantino, Quentin, 26, 32, 45
technological development, 65
Tell No One, 55–57, 60, 100
Thomas, Rob, 45
Tragic Thrills, 88
Troma company,
Tumblr, 53
Twentieth Century Fox, 31
Twitter, 53

Tylko nie mów nikomu, 55–57, 60, 100
typology of crowdfunding, 7
Tzioumakis, Yannis, 18, 24–28, 33, 36, 38

van Dijck, José, 58
Veronica Mars, 13, 42, 45
video to promote project, 14
VOD platforms, competitiveness of, 28

Warner Bros, 32, 42
Washington, Denzel, 47
Waters, John, 26
websites, use of, 4, 6, 44, 50, 53–54, 74, 78, 92
winner-take-all markets, 99
Wish I Was Here, 45, 48
Worldview Entertainment, 46

YouTube, 54, 59–60, 91

For Product Safety Concerns and Information please contact our EU representative GPSR@taylorandfrancis.com
Taylor & Francis Verlag GmbH, Kaufingerstraße 24, 80331 München, Germany